W9-CJZ-091

Lies Girls Believe is a fantastic tool for moms to ⟨⟩ ▭▭▭ strong against the lies they will be tempted to believe in their teens and twenties and beyond. Invest in your daughter's future by equipping her with Truth. Because the old saying got it right—an ounce of prevention is *definitely* worth a pound of cure!

MARY A. KASSIAN
Author of *Girls Gone Wise*

I loved *Lies Young Women Believe* by Nancy DeMoss Wolgemuth and Dannah Gresh. And now, I am so excited to see *Lies Girls Believe* introduce younger girls to the Truth that sets them free. Only Jesus can do that, but Dannah makes understanding how to experience it so accessible. I can't wait to get it into the hands of my granddaughters!

CATHE LAURIE
Founder and director of Virtue, the women's ministry at Harvest Christian Fellowship

Our daughters are being surrounded by positive sounding messages like "Girl Boss" and "Girls Rule the World." But is that the Truth? No—the Truth is that *Jesus* is the boss and He rules! I'm so glad Dannah Gresh has written this guide for moms to combat the lies of social media, pop culture, and foolish friends. Grab your daughter and this book, and head to a favorite spot to talk. I know this book will be the conversation starter for many intentional dates with my daughters!

ARLENE PELLICANE
Speaker and author of *Parents Rising* and *31 Days to Becoming a Happy Mom*

Girls have never had a more fun way to discover Truth and help them recognize the lies that break trust and relationships. Dannah Gresh clearly compares the lies to Truth in ways girls can identify to correct beliefs about themselves and discover Christ's goal for their life.

RON HUNTER JR.
Cofounder and director of the D6 Conference
Author of *DNA of D6: Building Blocks of Generational Discipleship*

Our girls' lives depend on their mothers knowing God's Truth. That sounds like a cliché, but for me it was and is still paramount to saving my daughter's life. Dannah unfolds a process that sets the mother-daughter team free to dispel lies and uncover the Truth God wants us to believe about His love for us, our families, friendships, and our future. You'll learn how to listen, dwell, believe, and act on God's Truth. Therein is freedom.

JENNY SUMMERS
Executive Director of Pregnancy Resource Clinic and mother of eight

A Mom's Guide to

Lies GIRLS Believe

& THE TRUTH THAT SETS THEM FREE

A Mom's Guide to Lies GIRLS Believe

& THE TRUTH THAT SETS THEM FREE

Dannah Gresh

FOREWORD BY NANCY DeMOSS WOLGEMUTH
LIES WE BELIEVE SERIES EDITOR

MOODY PUBLISHERS
CHICAGO

Unless otherwise indicated, all Scripture quotations are taken from the Holy Bible, New Living Translation, copyright © 1996, 2004, 2015 by Tyndale House Foundation. Used by permission of Tyndale House Publishers, Inc., Carol Stream, Illinois 60188. All rights reserved.

Scripture quotations marked ESV are taken from the The Holy Bible, English Standard Version® (ESV®) Copyright © 2001 by Crossway, a publishing ministry of Good News Publishers. All rights reserved. ESV Text Edition: 2016

Scripture quotations marked NKJV are taken from the New King James Version®. Copyright © 1982 by Thomas Nelson. Used by permission. All rights reserved.

Scripture quotations marked NIV are taken from the Holy Bible, NEW INTERNATIONAL VERSION®, NIV® Copyright © 1973, 1978, 1984, 2011 by Biblica, Inc.® Used by permission. All rights reserved worldwide.

Scripture quotations marked NIrV are taken from the Holy Bible, New International Reader's Version®, NIrV® Copyright © 1995, 1996, 1998, 2014 by Biblica, Inc.™ Used by permission of Zondervan. All rights reserved worldwide. www.zondervan.com The "NIrV" and "New International Reader's Version" are trademarks registered in the United States Patent and Trademark Office by Biblica, Inc.™

All emphasis in Scripture has been added.

Some names and details have been changed to protect the privacy of individuals.

Edited by Ashleigh Slater
Lies We Believe Series Editor: Nancy DeMoss Wolgemuth
Interior Design & Ilustrations: Julia Ryan/www.DesignByJulia
Cover Design: Erik M. Peterson
Cover Image: Cover photo of candy apple copyright © 2018 Yastremska/Bigstock (200730625). All rights reserved.
Photo/Image Credits: candy apple copyright © 2018 Yastremska/Bigstock (200730625). All rights reserved pgs 5, 21, 55, 179; © Photography by Britton (photographybybritton.com) p 11; © Jason Nelson p 67; © Douglas Saum p 99
Author photo: Steve Smith

Library of Congress Cataloging-in-Publication Data

Names: Gresh, Dannah, 1967- author. | Gresh, Dannah, 1967- Lies girls believe.
Title: A mom's guide to lies girls believe : and the truth that sets them
   free / Dannah Gresh.
Description: Chicago : Moody Publishers, 2019. | Includes bibliographical
   references. | Description based on print version record and CIP data
   provided by publisher; resource not viewed.
Identifiers: LCCN 2018050636 (print) | LCCN 2019004342 (ebook) | ISBN
   9780802492579 () | ISBN 9780802414298
Subjects: LCSH: Mothers and daughters--Religious aspects--Christianity. |
   Gresh, Dannah, 1967- Lies girls believe. | Preteen girls--Religious life.
   | Truthfulness and falsehood--Religious aspects--Christianity.
Classification: LCC BV4529.18 (ebook) | LCC BV4529.18 .G739 2019 (print) |
   DDC 248.8/431--dc23
LC record available at https://lccn.loc.gov/2018050636

ISBN: 978-0-8024-1429-8

We hope you enjoy this book from Moody Publishers. Our goal is to provide high-quality, thought-provoking books and products that connect truth to your real needs and challenges. For more information on other books and products written and produced from a biblical perspective, go to www.moodypublishers.com or write to:

Moody Publishers
820 N. LaSalle Boulevard
Chicago, IL 60610

3 5 7 9 10 8 6 4

Printed in the United States of America

CONTENTS

🍎

PART 1:
GETTING READY TO HELP YOUR DAUGHTER
(Dismantling Three Lies Moms Believe)

🍎

PART 2:
LIES GIRLS BELIEVE AND THE TRUTH THAT SETS THEM FREE
(Planting Seeds of Truth in Your Daughter's Life)

🍎

PART 3:
THE TRUTH THAT SETS HER FREE
(How to Identify Lies and Replace Them with Truth)

Nancy

From my heart to yours . . .

When I first wrote *Lies Women Believe* in 2001, my burden was particularly for adult women who had fallen prey to the deception of the enemy. As women read the book, many shared with me that the lies they believed had been rooted in their thinking since their teen years. It became increasingly clear that we needed to address these issues in younger women, before those lies could take root and produce destructive results in their lives. So in 2008, I invited Dannah Gresh to join me in penning *Lies Young Women Believe*.

It didn't occur to me back then that one day we would need another version of the book to help even younger girls recognize and overcome lies. At that point, these girls weren't yet on the front lines of the battle, as teens were. They weren't manifesting the telltale consequences of believing lies that their moms and grandmoms were experiencing.

But all that was changing while Dannah and I were writing the book for teenagers. The word "tween"—first coined in the 1940s—finally gained popular usage to describe the new consumer demographic of eight-to-twelve-year olds. They were being targeted in an effort to widen the market on products once sold to adults and teens. Suddenly things like makeup and brand name fashion were "necessary" for girls. The results were measurable and almost immediate: depression, body image issues, and eating disorders skyrocketed among these girls, many of whom had not yet reached puberty. And the problem has only worsened in the last decade or so.

There are two important reasons for our decision to extend the line of *Lies* books beyond women and young women, to include girls.

1. Tween girls are being targeted with mature content by the world.

To the mom holding this book who wants to shelter her daughter from the lies of this world, I empathize. Though I don't have any biological daughters, there are many precious young women and girls I claim as "adopted" children and, now, grandkids. (Several of these little ones served as bell-ringers in my wedding!) I wish they never had to witness firsthand the sin and ugliness in our broken world.

But our once Judeo-Christian culture is now fully post-Christian, and is intent on indoctrinating us from the cradle to the grave with its deceptive ways of thinking. There is no escaping it.

I'll be honest—I flinched when I learned that in addition to topics like beauty, friendship, academic pressure, and boys, Dannah felt we also needed to address things like social media, gender, and homosexuality. Many questions raced through my mind: *Was it really necessary to address these issues? Were girls really aware of and struggling with them? Could we write about them without prematurely exposing these young hearts to topics they weren't developmentally ready to handle?*

As you'll soon see, the research convinced me something had to be done. I am grateful for Dannah's commitment to safeguard these young hearts and minds—not by introducing them to *lies*, but by immersing them in the *Truth*.

Sheltering these precious girls from learning about these difficult issues is no longer possible. That's why we must do all we can to help them know and believe what God says.

2. Tween girls can experience life-shaping spiritual formation

It's easy to discount the childhood years, not realizing they are an important season of spiritual formation. Moms want to be sure their children are growing physically at the appropriate rate. And kids today are encouraged to develop and excel as students or athletes or musicians, and in their social skills. But are we as intentional about the development of their hearts and their relationship with God?

Jesus' life models spiritual formation from a young age, as He "grew in wisdom and stature, and in favor with God and man" (Luke 2:52). That's the way we are all supposed to grow—as a whole person, body, soul, spirit. Your daughter really can experience life-directing growth of her soul and spirit, even if she is young.

When I was just seven years old, I wrote a letter to my parents that reflected seeds they and others had planted in my heart. (Dannah has included it in your daughter's book on page 131, and you'll find it on page 173 in this *Mom's Guide*.) The original letter is in childlike handwriting with misspellings and all, but there was a distinct point at which I had sensed that God wanted me to be "a missionary for Him," and I was eager to share this wonderful news with my parents.

Some sweet friends had this letter framed for me when I turned forty, and it still sits in my living room—a reminder of God's call in my life, which I first experienced as a young girl. I vividly recall that clear sense that God owned my life, that my life belonged to Him, and that I had been set apart to be used by Him in His kingdom.

I don't know what God may have in store for your daughter. But I do know that what she thinks, believes, and does at the age of eight and ten matters. It matters that she is growing to know and love God with all her heart, and that she is learning to discern and hold steadfastly to Truth.

Lies Girls Believe and this *Mom's Guide* are tools to help you to plant Truth into your daughter, and to nurture those seeds and watch them grow. Parenting your daughter well in these formative years is time-consuming, hard work. But be assured that whatever time and effort you invest in her life now will bear fruit for years—and generations—to come!

May the Lord give you much wisdom and grace for this noble calling. And may He fill you with joy as you and your daughter savor together the beauty and power of the Truth.

NANCY DEMOSS WOLGEMUTH
Lies We Believe Series Editor
Author; teacher/host of Revive Our Hearts

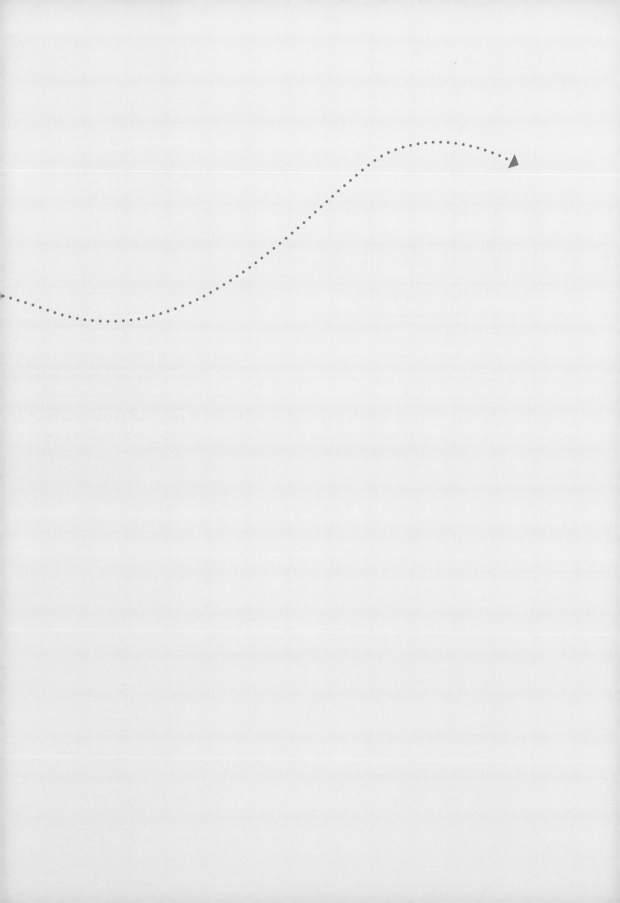

INTRODUCTION

What Every Mom Needs to Know about Her Daughter's Emotions

ere's a fun question to start a conversation with your daughter: What's the largest living organism in the world? Your first thought may be a blue whale—but that's not the correct answer! It's a tree in the Fishlake National Forest in Utah that's so big it even has a name: Pando. And it's not a giant sequoia, commonly known as a redwood. It's an aspen tree, more specifically a clonal colony of an individual male quaking aspen.*

Pando, also known as the Trembling Giant, looks like a forest of trees. But genetic markers have been identified in each tree trunk proving that they share one massive underground root system. The plant spreads across 106 acres and is thought to weigh 6,600 *tons*. (That's about 33 blue whales!)

And here's something about this tree that I find especially interesting: it has survived frequent forest fires because of its deep, wide-spreading roots. When fires rage through Pando, its root system is protected from the heat. The underground life source of the organism thrives and eventually sends new seedlings up into the fertile soil the fire leaves behind.

By contrast, conifers, which also grow in that area, have shallow root systems. When a fire comes through, it consumes these trees entirely.

Roots are powerful things.

The thing about roots, though, is that you can't see them. A tree may look strong and healthy from the surface, but you can't tell much about what's underground until the roots are tested.

What kind of roots does your daughter have? Are they deep and wide-spreading like Pando? Or shallow and weak like the roots of a conifer?

I know many parents who wish they could go back in time for another chance to establish the spiritual roots of their children. But it's too late. By their high school or college years, the sweet toddlers who once wore footie jammies have become a statistic of brokenness, sinfulness, or worse. Some don't have terrible manifestations of rejecting God, but they have settled into

* A clonal colony is a group of genetically identical individuals, such as plants, fungi, or bacteria that have grown in a given location, all originating vegetatively, not sexually, from a single ancestor.

the subtle neutrality of a "good" but godless life. Their roots were not deep enough.

Now, let me be clear. Godly parents do sometimes end up with ungodly children. The narrative of Adam and Eve proves this. But, that's not what I'm talking about here. What I am talking about are parents who *know* they could have done better. They tell me they were not as intentional to plant Truth, as they were to teach body care or nurture extracurricular interests. Regrets about placing too much importance on academics and not enough on spiritual character have mounted and become a painfully heavy burden. These parents now fervently pray as they wait for God to rescue their adult daughter miraculously.

I don't want this to be you. I'd like to help you with your daughter while she's still young. There are no guarantees, except that you'll know you have been intentional about planting Truth in her heart.

I've been through this with my two daughters, Lexi and Autumn. They are now twenty-somethings settling into the thrill of real-life "adulting." They aren't perfect, and wouldn't want me to tell you otherwise, but I'm happy to say we didn't just survive their tween and teen years. We thrived in them.

Of course, a lot has changed since they were that age. And, I wanted to be in touch with your parenting reality. So, I traveled across the country to facilitate focus groups with mothers of tween girls. Here are some things moms told me they were concerned about.

🍎 *My daughter learned about women's rights and abortion in fifth grade. Her public school teacher was a staunch feminist and integrated her political beliefs into the curriculum. I didn't know about things like that when I was her age.*

🍎 *There's more targeted advertising. Media giants decided they weren't making enough money, looked around, and identified the tween market. They especially target our girls. It used to be toys, but now it's makeup, food, [and] clothing. Our daughters think they need these things.*

🍎 *My daughter came home with a book from the library. It exalted the fact that the main character had two moms and met a boy who has two moms. I was disappointed that the public library had this agenda-pushing book available for my second grader.*

🍎 *She was in third grade and eight years old when a fifth grader committed suicide. I don't think children were committing suicide when I was that age.*

These mothers were seeking safe, age-appropriate ways to discuss mature and sensitive topics with their daughters. They wanted to do so without introducing them to confusing lies. Admittedly, these are subjects you and I would find challenging to navigate as grown women. So, how do you talk about them with a ten-year-old? And should you?

The decisions of how and when to bring up conversations are further complicated by how incredibly emotional the tween years can be. The words mothers used to describe their daughters included *insecure, embarrassed, confused, stressed out, angry, depressed, ashamed,* and *lonely.* They kept asking me if the reactions their daughters were having to life were developmentally normal, or something to be concerned about. That's a critical question with no simple answer. Each mother has to answer it for herself. But I've developed a tool to help you.

I coined the term *sticky feelings* to give you and your daughter something to identify unhealthy emotions. I've tested it out with high school and college-aged girls, and think it's something all of us can use to decide if our emotional reactions are healthy or if they are a warning sign that something is wrong.

STICKY FEELINGS

Your daughter's sweet little body is going to be or already has begun experiencing an onslaught of hormonal complications that make discerning healthy and unhealthy emotions difficult. But it can be done.

In the introduction to *Lies Girls Believe*, I wrote this for your daughter:

> God created both good and bad feelings, and they can both be useful if you use God's Truth to respond to them. But when you have a bad feeling and you don't know why, or it just never goes away and you feel it all the time, EVERY DAY, that's a "sticky" feeling. It may be evidence that you believe a lie!

It's entirely possible that your daughter is struggling with a particular emotion because God needs her—with your help—to respond in Truth. Maybe she is stressed out because there is too much on her schedule, and you need to help her make room for rest. Perhaps she is depressed because she doesn't feel safe talking about things that make her angry, and she needs to learn how to communicate her frustrations in a mature way. God created our emotions to send us messages, and we're supposed to respond to those signals. When we do, the feeling often departs because it has done its work.

But sometimes, emotions stick to a girl. They show up for no apparent reason and/or they never leave! That's when you might have a problem. Here's what every mother needs to know about her daughter's emotions:

Chronic, recurrent, sticky feelings could be evidence that lies are growing in the roots of your daughter's belief system. She could be in spiritual bondage.

The term *spiritual bondage*, which Nancy DeMoss Wolgemuth used in *Lies Woman Believe* to describe what Christian adult women experience, also explains the crisis tween girls are facing. Seventy-two percent of the moms who attended my focus groups said they believe their daughter's emotions are a manifestation of a much deeper, darker battle. One mother put it this way:

"Satan does not discriminate based on age."

I agree.

You probably picked up this book because you do too.

But where do we begin to help our precious girls?

Through Nancy's book *Lies Women Believe: And the Truth That Sets Them Free*, over one million women have experienced victory over all manner of sin, depression, anxiety, fear, loneliness, addiction, hopelessness, and so much more. She's helped readers trace their spiritual bondage to deeply-rooted lies. Then, she's helped them rip up the lies and replace them with God's Truth.

OUR DAUGHTERS HAVE BEEN LIED TO. THEY NEED TRUTH TO SET THEM FREE.

The *Lies Girls Believe* and *Mom's Guide to Lies Girls Believe* set of books is the answer to the groundswell of mothers requesting a similar book for their eight- to twelve-year-old daughters. What if I told you that instead of being jealous, mean, moody, greedy, and in bondage, your daughter could grow up to be:

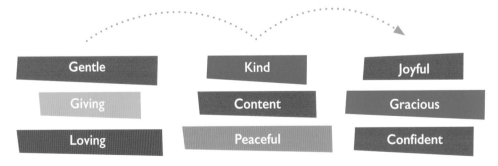

Gentle	Kind	Joyful
Giving	Content	Gracious
Loving	Peaceful	Confident

This is how God intended her—and you—to live: *free*. Of course, Jesus told us it would not be easy. He said: ▼

TRUTH NUGGET: "[Satan]'s purpose is to steal and kill and destroy. My purpose is to give [you] a rich and satisfying life." (John 10:10)

There are going to be tough battles in your daughter's life as Satan seeks to lie to her, and God wants her to know and believe Truth. I want to help you and your daughter win the war, so you can experience the abundant life that Jesus came to give both of you. You cannot choose whether your daughter will embrace God's Word, but you can plant seeds in her so she is rooted in Truth.

The writers of the Old Testament understood the importance of being well rooted. Jeremiah, Ezekiel, and the Psalmists all wrote about it. The Apostle Paul leaned on their words when he wrote: ▼

TRUTH NUGGET: "Therefore, as you received Christ Jesus the Lord, so walk in him, rooted and built up in him and established in the faith, just as you were taught, abounding in thanksgiving." (Colossians 2:6–7 ESV)

My goal in this book and *Lies Girls Believe* is to help you plant seeds and nurture deep, wide-spread roots of Truth in your daughter.

What do you say, friend? Let's get planting.

HOW TO USE *LIES GIRLS BELIEVE* AND A MOM'S GUIDE TO *LIES GIRLS BELIEVE* TOGETHER

1 READ *A Mom's Guide to Lies Girls Believe* at the same time/pace that your daughter reads *Lies Girls Believe*. So, when you read this introduction, you should also prompt your daughter to read the introduction in her book. The chapters parallel one another and set you up for great mother–daughter conversations.

2 PRAY for your daughter. I'll provide prayer ideas in each chapter in this book. They'll look like this:

TALKING WITH GOD:

Use John 10:10 to write a prayer for your daughter below. Ask God to make you a wise mother who sees when Satan is trying to steal your daughter's heart. Pray that God will use this book to equip you to help your daughter enjoy a rich and satisfying life in Christ.

[Satan]'s purpose is to steal and kill and destroy.
My purpose is to give [you] a rich and satisfying life. (John 10:10)

---

3 **TALK** with your daughter. Use the conversation suggestions at the end of your chapter to talk with your daughter. They will look like this:

TALKING WITH YOUR GIRL:

After your daughter reads the introduction to *Lies Girls Believe*, have her turn to page 16 and ask if she is willing to discuss her answers to the Girl Drama Quiz. This is your chance to discern further where she needs your prayers and guidance.

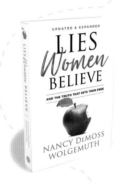

LIES WOMEN BELIEVE

I encourage you to begin by reading and applying the Truth found in Nancy's book *Lies Women Believe*. If you've read it previously, you might consider skimming through it again, so it's fresh in your mind. There is no greater tool you can give your daughter to experience Truth and freedom than having a life-transforming encounter with Truth yourself.

PART
1

Getting Ready to Help Your Daughter

(Dismantling Three Lies Moms Believe)

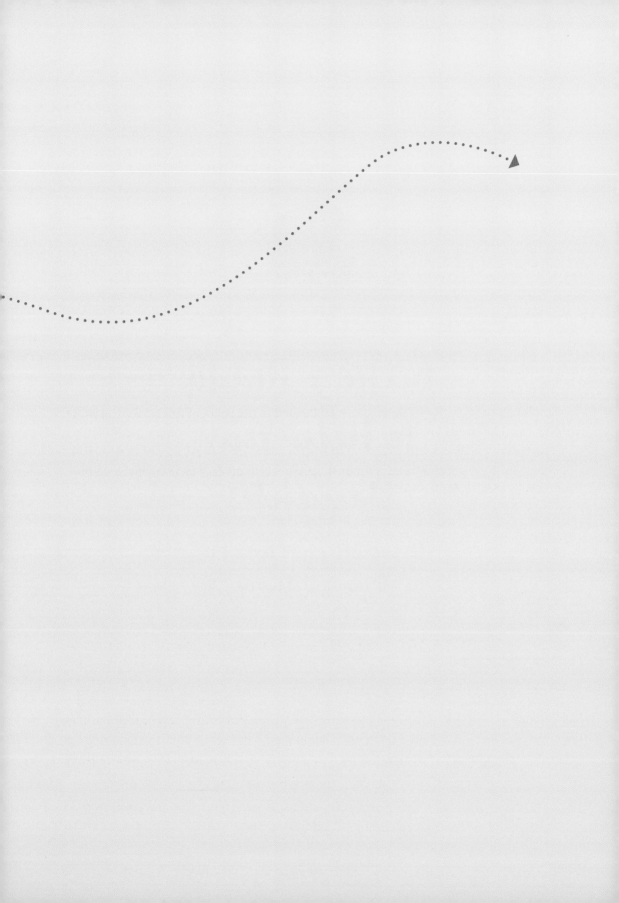

Dannah

To gather stories for this book, I hit the road, made coffee, and had conversations with mothers of tween girls in eleven cities.

156 WOMEN
PARTICIPATED IN OUR FOCUS GROUPS!

At each of these events, women held voting clickers. I asked them a question such as, *"Is your daughter boy crazy?"* Each attendee answered privately, giving me a baseline percentage of how widespread a problem might be. Then, we'd talk it out. Our conversations often became tear-filled and cathartic, as women shared their saddest stories and deepest fears about motherhood. We were also often encouraged, as women shared their victories in the battle for Truth.

You'll find their stories—case studies—embedded in the pages of this book. The names are fictional. The stories are not.

These moms helped me to pinpoint the lies addressed in the next section of this book. Together, we also identified three lies moms believe which hinder our ability to teach our daughters to walk in Truth. They are:

▶ **MOM LIE #1:** "I can't/can control what my daughter believes."

▶ **MOM LIE #2:** "It's too soon to talk to my daughter about _____."

▶ **MOM LIE #3:** "My daughter is not at risk like other girls."

If these sentences sound all-too-uncomfortably accurate, lean in for some comfort and direction. You're not alone.

If you really don't think they fit you, could I ask you—dare you—to read the next few chapters anyway? I hope you prove me wrong, but I'll be the first to admit I didn't think I had embraced these lies. Upon examining my heart, I realized I either had or still was letting them manifest in my life. And, I don't know about you, but I don't want anything to prevent me from helping my girls live in the freedom of Truth! So, before we help your daughter, I'd like to spend some time encouraging and supporting you in the next three chapters.

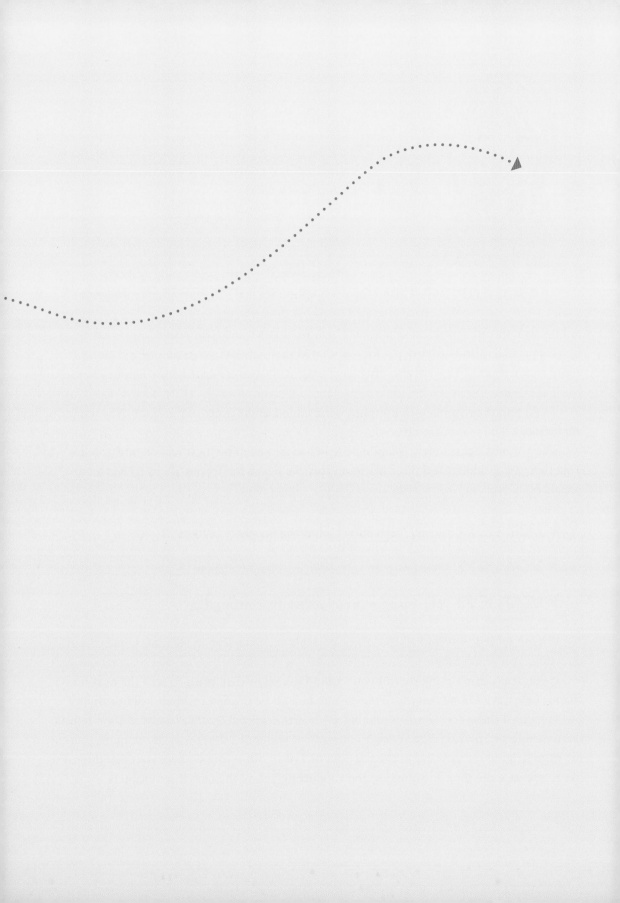

You Have a Decision to Make

Two photos are forever cemented into my mind.

The first one is a precious image of a girl I know kneeling with her mom, who is my friend, to surrender her life to Christ. In this photo, the girl—whose name I simply cannot get myself to fictionalize—has a smile so big it's contagious.

The other photo is horrific. It is of the same girl. Let me tell you a little more about my friend and her daughter, before I tell you what the image looks like.

When she was eleven, she began to pressure her parents for permission to have an Instagram account. But they maintained that the app's minimum recommended age[1] should be respected. They stood firm and told her "not yet." When their daughter had a strong emotional reaction to their decision, they thought it was just "normal" tween-girl drama.

After all, even after her request, she continued to be involved in and succeed in a lot of extracurricular activities, remained a helpful big sister, and still melted hearts when she sang. She seemed to have accepted their "not yet."

Nothing could have prepared them for the phone call they got some months later from a neighbor, to warn them of their daughter's secret. She had gone behind her parents' backs to open an Instagram account.

But that wasn't the worst of it.

Her most recent post was a chilling photo I wish I had never seen. This precious girl, not yet twelve years old, had cuts in her wrist and blood was running down her arm as she stared blankly into the camera.

My friend had a decision to make: how would she use this painful opportunity to nurture her daughter in Truth?

I'm guessing you picked up this book for the same reason I wrote it. You see that our girls are in trouble, and you want to do something about it.

Most of today's tween girls suffer on what is called a spectrum of angst. It's not a matter of *if* they will struggle—with depression, anxiety, fear, loneliness, and anger—but *how much*. Sociologist Juliet Schor, who studies trends in family and women's issues, warns that the emotional problems manifesting in our daughters that may seem normal to us were cause for aggressive treatment not so many years ago.

> *Today's average (i.e., normal) young person between the ages of nine and seventeen scores as high on anxiety scales as children who were admitted to clinics for psychiatric disorders in 1957.*[2]

In an effort to keep their daughters from being a statistic, many moms are leaning on bestselling books, counseling, mommy blogs, and popular speakers to help them. There's often nothing wrong with these resources. In fact, I've used all of them to help me become a healthier woman and to raise whole children. They offer us understanding and good ideas, but on their own, they do not get to the heart of solving the brokenness in our families.

Friend, we need more than just talking about the ruin that is occurring in tween girls. We need a solution. We need to understand *WHY* they are struggling and *HOW* to stop it.

WHY GIRLS ARE STRUGGLING

As your daughter is learning in chapter 1 of *Lies Girls Believe*, all of our troubles go back to the Garden of Eden where Satan, disguised as a snake, told the very first lie to the very first woman. From that encounter until now, he has used deception to win our affections, influence our choices, and ultimately destroy our lives. ▼

 TRUTH NUGGET: "The devil . . . was a murderer from the beginning. He has always hated the truth, because there is no truth in him. When he lies, it is consistent with his character; for he is a liar and the father of lies." (John 8:44)

Lying has always been Satan's game plan.

But here's the thing: We play the game with him. Eve wasn't a completely innocent bystander. She cooperated with the snake.

How did Eve go from having a perfect day in Paradise to the most cataclysmic day in all of human history? She listened to the snake's lie, and then she began to dwell on it. She mulled it over and got emotional, which is what led to her downfall. When obsessive thoughts and emotions take over, we are in deep trouble. I wrote it like this for your daughter:

Maybe she **FELT** confused.

"Wait . . . did Adam misunderstand what God told him?!"

Or maybe she **FELT** rebellious.

"If that's how God is going to be, I don't *want* to follow God's rules!"

Or maybe she **FELT** afraid.

"Oh no! What if God isn't as good as we think He is?"

We don't know what Eve was thinking or feeling, but we can see that she allowed her feelings to be in control. That's when something really bad happened: **Eve began to believe the lie.** She questioned God's Truth!

THE WOMAN BELIEVED THE LIE

Believing the lie led to eating the fruit God told her and Adam not to eat. The consequences of that sin have known no end. Here are some of the alarming ways they are manifesting as risks to our daughters today:

- 🍎 *Adolescent depression rates are on the rise, with tween girls especially at risk.[3]*

- 🍎 *An increase in reported anxiety, sleeplessness, loneliness, worry, and dependence coincides with the release of the first smartphone.[4] 23.5 million users of Snapchat are under the age of eleven.[5]*

🍎 *Rates of ER visits for treatment of cutting, burning, and ingesting poison has surged almost 19 percent between 2009 and 2015 for girls aged ten to fourteen.*[6]

🍎 *The average age of onset for anorexia has dropped from thirteen to seventeen down to nine to twelve, with children as young as seven being diagnosed. Sixty percent of elementary and middle school teachers witness eating disorders in their schools.*[7]

While many girls won't show up in the scary stats above, most will struggle with body image issues, mean-girl moments, boy craziness, materialism, academic pressure, and a host of other more common problems.

We've got to do something.

HOW TO HELP THEM

There is something more powerful than Satan's lies— and that is God's Truth.

For over two decades, I have been guiding teens and adult women through recovery of all kinds of emotional trauma, addictions, and sinful patterns. I have helped them realize what lies they have believed and how to experience dramatic Truth encounters with God's Spirit. It is always breathtaking to see Him at work.

This process works for younger girls too. And it's time to begin to use it. The lies girls believe must be uprooted and replaced with God's Truth. This is the skill I want to help your daughter learn in the pages of *Lies Girls Believe*.

I'm not talking about a mystical formula that will make all her tween drama disappear. There won't be any shortcuts past mean girls, school stress, or family pain. Life is hard. But together, you and I can equip your daughter to walk through the realities of life—academic stress, peer pressure, social media angst, getting cut from a team, and even family brokenness— in freedom and true joy.

But, before we get to the Truth your daughter needs, do you mind if we talk about some Truth that you and I need?

Let's lean into Genesis 3—the same passage your daughter is studying in *Lies Girls Believe*— to conform our hearts to Truth. After all, just because we are moms does not mean we don't have any sticky feelings, or that we have become immune to lies.

IN THE FIRST THREE CHAPTERS OF THIS BOOK, I'D LIKE TO UNPACK THREE OF THE BIGGEST LIES MOMS BELIEVE. LET'S DIVE INTO THE FIRST.

It's one that I know very well.

There were times of mothering my tween girls when I *felt* a deep sense of impotence, almost as if I was comatose and could not imagine what to say or do. For example, when they faced friendship drama, I sometimes felt clueless about how to sort it out. Or when they wanted to buy that cute but short pair of cut-offs, I struggled with how to say "no," without sounding self-righteous or implying that this was a measurement of their spirituality or mine. The confusion overwhelmed me. I sometimes felt like there was no way to control what my daughters believed.

Then, there were those euphoric times when I *felt* like I deserved the "Christian Mother of the Year" award. I felt superior to other mothers and believed I was in control of my daughters' beliefs. Don't judge! You know you've been there too.

Note the emphasis on my feelings. Just like Eve—and our daughters—you and I are prone to allow our feelings to control us. The emotions I had concerning my daughters' developing belief systems and my parenting skills were evidence that I was struggling with a common mom lie.

▶ MOM LIE #1: ◀
"I CAN'T/CAN CONTROL WHAT MY DAUGHTER BELIEVES."

This lie—actually two variations of the same lie—is powerful and preeminent, which is why you'll also find it addressed in *Lies Women Believe.* The first version of it tells us that we have no control. The second tells us that we have supreme control.

The Enemy uses these two polar opposites to place us in bondage as moms. One causes complacency because we are fearful that our intervention wouldn't help anyway. The other causes pride that we have everything under control, causing us to miss important cues when our daughters are in trouble.

I had one particularly perplexing encounter with a mother who never made it to one of my focus groups. She's an articulate, intelligent woman whose opinions I was excited to hear for my research. When I saw her at a public event, I told her as much. She kindly explained that she would not be attending my focus group. I asked her why. She said, *"My daughter is home-schooled. I monitor the influences in her life, so she doesn't believe any lies."*

I stared blankly at her, unsure of what to say. Positive I had misunderstood or that she had misspoken, I asked her to clarify. And she did. She was confident her daughter was not at risk.

Though that is an extreme example, I have found many moms who believe the lie that they cannot control or that they do control what their daughter believes.

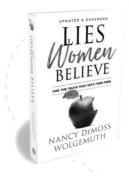

Can you really control how your daughter turns out? Read Nancy's thoughts in chapter 8 of *Lies Women Believe.*

Consider this: *What's the difference between being responsible for nurturing your daughter in Truth and controlling her behavior?*

The Truth is that God wants you to do everything you can to plant seeds of Truth in your daughter. No matter how overwhelmed you may feel by her behavior or circumstances, you are charged with the task of being faithful to present Truth. In a key Old Testament passage, the Scripture emphasizes how intentionally and carefully we must approach the work of teaching Truth to our children. ▼

 TRUTH NUGGET: "Repeat them again and again to your children. Talk about them when you are at home and when you are on the road, when you are going to bed and when you are getting up. Tie them to your hands and wear them on your forehead as reminders. Write them on the doorposts of your house and on your gates." (Deuteronomy 6:7–9)

This may not be easy for you. Like me, you'll have days where you feel ill-equipped for the issue at hand. Even in the best of circumstances, you may face challenges.

But some moms have special hardships. For example, in the focus groups we conducted for this book, many shed tears as they spoke of having daughters whose fathers—sometimes in the home and sometimes not—were unbelievers. One stepmother told me that her eleven-year-old daughter spends half of her life in her home, and half of the time with her biological mom who is an atheist. The girl is often told that Christianity is "a crutch" for weak people.

Don't let your emotions cause you to parent out of fear. Yes, Truth will always have enemies and opposition, but don't let that stop you from planting Truth in your girl.

God took the time to make sure Adam and Eve knew the truth about the tree, knowing Satan would lie to them. He even told them of the dire consequences of failing to obey Him. ▼

 TRUTH NUGGET: "You may freely eat the fruit of every tree in the garden—except the tree of the knowledge of good and evil. If you eat its fruit, you are sure to die." (Genesis 2:16–17)

God planted Truth in His precious first son and daughter.

I know that sometimes your emotions feel conflicted when you have to do the same. Have you ever considered how the God of the Universe may have felt when He spoke those words to His children? God's emotions are never expressed sinfully, with distortion, or outside of His holiness, but He does feel. Was there some sadness within Him when He spoke these words, knowing Satan would come with the lies? And yet, He spoke the Truth, nonetheless.

It is crucial for us to follow this example and tell our children about the temptations we know they will face. In the pages of *Lies Girls Believe*, I've tried to bring some of those topics up in a safe environment where you can be in the driver's seat of presenting Truth to your daughter. In the first chapter, your daughter meets a fictional girl named Zoey.

Zoey is facing the temptation to get on social media behind her parents' backs. She has her own form of the Tree of Knowledge of Good and Evil. Her parents have allowed many ways for her to connect with her friends, but social media is one form of connection that they think she is not ready to experience yet.

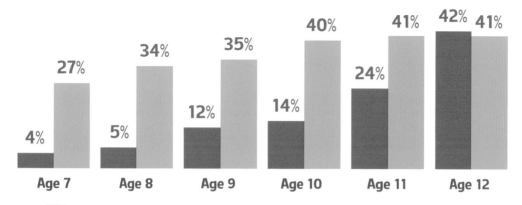

	Age 7	Age 8	Age 9	Age 10	Age 11	Age 12
With Internet	4%	5%	12%	14%	24%	42%
iPad or Tablet	27%	34%	35%	40%	41%	41%

■ Tween Girls Who Report Having Smartphones **With Internet**

■ Tween Girls Who Report Having Their Own Personal iPad or Tablet

Based on our Lies Girls Believe survey of 1,531 girls aged 7–12, 69% of whom claimed to be Christians. Presumed to be predominately from active evangelical Christian homes.

Let me be honest with you: there were lengthy conversations with the publishing team about whether or not to include social media as a prominent storyline at the beginning of your daughter's book. It was a difficult decision because we all agreed that if your daughter is under the age of thirteen, she does not have the developmental and emotional maturity required to navigate social media. (And, sometimes then, it is still too soon.) Even the creators of the social media apps themselves set recommended age limits, usually stating that an individual cannot create an account before the age of thirteen. Those restrictions exist for a reason.

If you are a mom who has respected the recommended age limits, I applaud you. It's not easy. You're swimming upstream. One mom said, "Most of my daughter's eleven-year-old friends have Instagram accounts, but I'm holding out. I feel like I'm all alone."

It may feel like it, but you're not alone. There are many moms still respecting the suggested age restrictions. And all moms should consider them.

If your daughter is on social media, I plead with you to carefully consider the impact it can have on her. Since its debut into pop culture, it has severely increased problems girls were already facing, including but not limited to

Hi! I'm Zoey!

A CASE STUDY:
CANDACE

Candace wanted Snapchat. She kept bringing it up to her parents, making a logical case for why she needed it. But her parents told her "no" several times. They were resolute, believing that she was not old enough.

Eventually, the pleading stopped, and Candace's parents were relieved that their daughter had finally dropped the topic.

But, one day, she left her phone on the kitchen counter. As her mom walked by, it lit up and vibrated. Glancing down, her mom read the message: "Jason accepts your invitation to Snapchat."

Her mom said, "She was completely deceptive! She even lied to me when I confronted her about it. I can hardly wrap my head around it."

body-image issues. The number one eating disorder clinic in the nation released this information in a statement about how the media impacts the risk of a girl having an eating disorder:

In early 2016, scientists reported evidence linking the use of social media with body image issues in young people. This included dieting, body surveillance, a strong desire for thinness and self-objectification. Although social media sites are not the cause of eating disorders, they are a factor in the development of body image issues.[8]

The two most popular apps among teen girls right now—Instagram and Snapchat—are causing a lot of sticky feelings that make girls feel depressed, ugly, and stressed. There is even a new word in the dictionary—FOMO—to describe the Fear Of Missing Out that many girls experience when they see their friends included in things when they are not.

Since I don't think your daughter should be on social media, it might seem odd that I chose to use this storyline in her book. Here's the thing: I heard story after story of moms begging me to sound an alarm. One of them was a mom who told me the account in the first case study to the left. It is the basis for Zoey's storyline.

In the end, the topic of social media use made it into your daughter's book because I believe that you and I must proactively talk to our daughters about the temptations we know exist. Just as God spoke to Adam and Eve about the temptation they would face in the Garden of Eden and what would happen if they didn't respect it, we should also speak to our girls about Truth and the consequences of ignoring it. Social media is only one of many important subjects we'll cover with your daughter as we seek to plant Truth deep into her being.

While you are responsible to plant seeds of Truth, it is also true that you are not in control of your daughter's belief system. One day she will stand before God and give account for her own beliefs (Deuteronomy 24:16; Jeremiah 31:29–30).

If the story of Adam and Eve demonstrates anything, it is this: God does not seek to restrain us. He could have built a wall to keep Adam and Eve from the Tree. He could have placed a canyon or moat around it. He could have caused the Tree not to blossom and grow fruit. There were many ways He could have controlled the outcome. He is God, and He is Sovereign. But He gave His children the freedom to choose between right and wrong. Why?

Because He wanted it to be real. He wanted their behavior to be an authentic reflection of their heart—of the roots beneath the fruit of their behavior.

Your daughter's behaviors—the things you can see— are the result of things you cannot see. Under the surface, her emotions are at work attempting to direct her life. But, as I will eventually explain in the last pages of *Lies Girls Believe*, her thoughts are "the boss of" her feelings. And, just under her thoughts, her beliefs are the roots in charge of everything.

BEHAVIORS
what people see

EMOTIONS
what we feel

THOUGHTS
what we think

BELIEFS
what we believe

Believing Truth is not merely agreeing with it. The Bible says that even the demons believe and shudder (James 2:19). And simply conforming our behavior to Truth is not sufficient. The Pharisees obeyed the rules faithfully, but Jesus called them "whitewashed tombs" (Matthew 23:27). They looked good on the outside, but on the inside . . . not so much.

I'm not saying that you should not control and direct your daughter's behavior. It is your responsibility to set healthy boundaries for her. Nothing concerns me more than when parents allow their children to call all the shots, as if they have no say in the matter. Your daughter is not ready to make most of her choices alone, such as when she'll date, what social media she'll have access to, what television and movies to watch, or even what kind of schooling is best for her. At this stage, she still needs you to help her make good choices, so she can slowly and steadily learn how to do it for herself as she moves toward adulthood.

IS YOUR DAUGHTER'S BEHAVIOR REAL?

In his dissertation entitled *The Nature of True Virtue*[8], Jonathan Edwards explains that there are two kinds of virtue. That is, there are two kinds of behavior that demonstrate high standards.

Common virtue is doing what is right but with false motives. You do the right thing out of fear, selfishness, or pride. For example, your daughter may be honest because she doesn't want to get in trouble. As we grow older, sometimes we're honest because we're prideful. We don't want to be like "those people" who are liars. This kind of virtue is not deeply rooted in Truth and seeks self-glory. Most people have common virtue.

True virtue is doing what is right because God is God. We are honest because God said to be. Period. This is rooted in God's Truth and is for His glory. Most people are willing to settle for the first form of virtue; few people pursue *true virtue*. But that should be what we are seeking to plant in our daughters.

But you can't *just* control and direct her. That's a recipe for trouble down the road. She needs to understand *why* you have established boundaries for her, and that happens as you plant seeds of Truth. There is a difference between simply controlling her behavior, and setting boundaries *while* you thoroughly nurture her in Truth.

Many of us face the risk of restraining our daughter's behavior out of fear. We work hard to control her behavior, so there is as little room as possible for failure. We try to keep sin and temptation far away from our families, and sometimes shelter our daughter so efficiently that she essentially becomes a monk. Simply restraining external behavior may seem efficient and easier in the short-run, but the long-term outcome is dubious because we haven't cultivated in her a love for Truth. We've essentially decreased the chances of her making wise behavioral choices when we aren't around.

💜 **A critical ingredient to nurturing your daughter with Truth is grace.**
In this model, you treat your daughter like God treated Eve. You plant Truth, but also expect the battle to be thick. You know your daughter will sin, and you prepare to respond with the same grace we have received from Christ. You talk openly about sin and temptation, and encourage your daughter to be involved in decision-making.

Nurturing a child in Truth is time-consuming and sometimes frustrating, but the long-term outcome is a young woman who has the roots of Truth established so she can make godly decisions even when you aren't there.

Will you be a mother who merely restrains your daughter's
external behavior so it appears to conform to Truth?

OR

Will you nurture her in Truth so that her external behavior
is an outgrowth of what is planted deep inside of her heart?

Which will it be?

The friend I mentioned at the beginning of this chapter was faced with that choice when she discovered her daughter had gotten on social media behind her back, and posted a photo of her own self-harm. Though everything in her wanted to respond in fearful control, instead she chose the more laborious approach to nurture her in Truth.

She began by asking her daughter what kind of thoughts she was thinking that led her to cut her wrist open. Her daughter tearfully began to speak mature, dark words. They were the words some boys at school had used as they bullied her, and words no girl should ever have to hear, but my friend's sweet daughter had begun to believe they might be true.

Then, my friend and her husband told their daughter that they needed help as a family. Within hours, their pastor was visiting to pray with and talk with them. They approached it as a family crisis, rather than just pointing fingers at their tween daughter.

Then began the long, hard on-going conversation to rip up lies by the root and plant Truth that heals.

Of course, there were some practical consequences and loss of privileges, but the focus was on this sweet little one's heart. Not her behavior.

As I write this almost one year has passed, and those two are still having a strong conversation as my friend nurtures her daughter in Truth.

TALKING WITH GOD:

Use Deuteronomy 6:6–9 to write a prayer to God. Examine your own heart and consider whether you are planting Truth in your daughter—and any other children in your home—as carefully and thoroughly as this verse commands. Write your honest petitions to God in the lines below.

Repeat them again and again to your children. Talk about them when you are at home and when you are on the road, when you are going to bed and when you are getting up. Tie them to your hands and wear them on your forehead as reminders. Write them on the doorposts of your house and on your gates. (Deuteronomy 6:7–9)

_____

_____

_____

_____

_____

TALKING WITH YOUR GIRL:

After your daughter reads chapter 1 in *Lies Girls Believe*, turn to page 24 and discuss her study of Genesis 3:1–7. Praise her if she has been diligent. Help her if she needs it.

Then, turn to page 29 where she wrote down what advice she would give Zoey about the temptation to disobey her parents. Discuss her ideas.

How to Nurture Your Daughter in Truth

I met Chloe when she was a sophomore in college. She came to me because she was performing oral sex on her boyfriend, even though she knew it was wrong. She told me she'd been having boundary issues with guys since she was in high school.

Many well-meaning Christian leaders would hear Chloe's confession, pray with her, and then offer advice about how to stop. Some would urge her to break up with the boy, at least for now. Others would offer to provide accountability: *I'm going to ask you the next time I see you if you've slipped.*

While those approaches are eventually helpful, it's not where I usually begin. I have never seen them successfully stop sin from sprouting back up. It's like cutting a dandelion off at the top without ripping up the roots. It will grow back.

That's why when someone like Chloe comes to me, I always try to go for the roots.

Sometimes the sin a girl is struggling with is rooted in something that might seem unrelated to the behavior itself. For that reason, I may spend a great deal of time meeting with her before I even guess what lies she might be believing.

Chloe was a true joy to get to know. Intelligent, funny, and genuine, she was a model Christian college student in every way. She got straight As, was a successful athlete, and actively served at her campus church.

I couldn't connect the dots, but God soon would. In a prayer time, we asked Him to help us see why Chloe was facing the same battle the Apostle Paul wrote about in Romans 7—doing what she didn't want to do, instead of doing what she wanted to do.

Soon, my friend looked up with tears in her eyes and told me a lie she'd believed since she was eight or nine years old.

"I have to perform to be loved."

The most important thing about our belief system is not our behavior. It's the roots.

The Bible uses the word *heart* to refer to the roots of our belief system. If you want to really influence thoughts, emotions, and behaviors, you can't focus your primary efforts on restraining them. You must impact a person's heart or belief system. The Bible communicates this Truth clearly.

> *As he thinks in his heart, so is he.*
> (Proverbs 23:7 NKJV)

When Eve ate the fruit, she proved what she believed deep down in her heart. When Chloe was performing fellatio on her boyfriend, she was proving what she really believed. It had less to do with what she thought about sex, and more to do with what she believed about performance. I helped her identify the lie and then gave her some biblical Truth to replace it.

I did not seek first and foremost to be an agent of restraint or accountability, but instead to rip up the lie and plant a seed of Truth within her.

When our daughters are mired in sticky feelings, exhibit harmful or sinful behavior, or deceive us, they are revealing the roots of lies. If you are intentional to nurture your daughter in Truth rather than simply restrain her outward behavior, you are developing an important tool. It will enable you to identify where the bad roots are growing, so you can help your daughter pull them up and replace them with Truth.

I have found that this complex process can freak a mom out! Restraining alone is so much easier, and you don't have to identify the lies that you wish were not there. For that reason, some moms pretend the evidence of the lies does not exist.

Can you say *fear*?

If you want to parent out of grace with the intention of nurturing Truth, you must first conquer your fear. Fear can cause us to be restrictive, legalistic, secretive, and overly sheltering.

To be clear, fear can be healthy. If you're chased by a grizzly bear, fear is good. But it can be dangerous and counterproductive when it comes to parenting.

Fear has a favorite subject to roll around in the minds of moms: their past. It often brings a buddy: unworthiness. These emotions make a big show of themselves when you think about discussing certain topics where you have believed—or still believe—lies. (Think: sex, gender, eating disorders, and depression.)

Some of the women in my focus groups claimed they weren't afraid of talking about those subjects, but had concerns about bringing up things their daughters weren't developmentally ready to process. That didn't surprise me, but what did was the fact that some of them included theology and spiritual formation on the list of off-limits topics. These mothers expressed a belief that allowing their daughters to make spiritual decisions too soon could result in the risk of the spiritual decisions not actually taking root. (That sounds a little like fear, doesn't it?)

As these conversations developed, other moms advocated for a different approach. They, too, had some fears. And some stories. Check out the case study of Angel to the right. ·········▶

So, who's right? The moms who are holding back or the moms who think we should discuss it all?

Well, only you can know for certain when your daughter is ready to tackle a topic.

But. . .

Let me be honest and maybe push you out of your comfort zone. I think a lot of moms who experience fear are believing this lie:

▶ MOM LIE #2: ◀
"IT'S TOO SOON TO TALK TO MY DAUGHTER ABOUT _____."

When we discussed this possibility, some mothers defended the fact that their daughters didn't yet believe lies in these off-limits topics. One mom explained her daughter's supposed resilience to lies this way: *"If I don't talk to my daughter about _____, a lie won't have the opportunity to present itself."*

Really? How do you know? If you haven't discussed something with her, how do really know what she does or doesn't believe?

I find that our daughters are usually ready to tackle scary topics much sooner than we are. Tween girls are at

A CASE STUDY:
ANGEL

Evonne's daughter, Angel, was in fourth grade when Evonne came home to find her little girl sitting on the sofa with her dad. He encouraged Angel to tell her mom what had happened.

"A friend had used the word *sex* at school," recalls Evonne. "She was curious so she came home and googled the word. She saw horrible things. She has seen sex in a horrible way."

Angel is not an isolated case. The word *sex* is the eleventh most searched word for children aged eight to twelve.[1]

Evonne expressed regret for having not started a conversation about sex earlier.

"Maybe if she had known a little more, she would have known to ask us," lamented the mother through tears. "If we don't tell them, the world will. *That's* what makes them lose innocence."

precisely the age when they are developmentally sorting through what they do and do not believe, and are likely eager for your tutoring. Let me show you what I mean.

STAGES OF MORAL DEVELOPMENT IN CHILDREN

For over two decades, I have studied the moral development of children. I did this as a mom and book geek. Without the P, h, and D behind my name, some of the language was complicated and unnecessary, so I developed my own terms for three stages of moral development. (You're welcome!)

THE COPYCAT PHASE (AGES 2-5)
Copying Beliefs

Children begin to develop their moral fabric from an early age. Between the ages of two and five, the primary way they form their beliefs is by imitating you. They are watching, observing, and copying you every moment of the day.

For this reason, your daughter will want everything you have like a cellphone or a little plastic kitchen. Her little heart is saying, *"Mommy does it. I want to be like Mommy because I like her. I'll do it, too!"* So, she cooks or works on her computer because she sees you do it. She also says "thank you" and is helpful or empathic because she's copying you. Obedience even becomes a little bit easier if she sees her mother modeling respect and responsiveness to others. (Ouch! I know. That one hurts a little, doesn't it? For the record, I just stepped on my own toes, not just yours.)

Little things matter. Showing affection to your husband in front of her begins to teach her the beauty of marriage. Returning extra change when the cashier makes a mistake—something I remember my mother doing—begins to teach her honesty. Saying things like, "It's great to be a girl," begins to form value for womanhood within her tender little system of Truth roots.

This phase of moral development is merely introductory. Nothing is cemented just yet, but exciting things can be happening if a mother pursues the planting and nurturing of Truth.

Of course, a newly developing belief system is terribly imperfect. The evidence of the roots being planted may even manifest in the most unusual way. During our focus groups, one mom shared an insightful story about her preschool daughter. Check out Chiosoka's case study to the left.

THE COUNSELING PHASE (AGES 6-11)
Considering Beliefs

Between the ages of six and eleven, your child is learning Truth by asking you *why* you believe what you believe and do what you do. This is an interactive phase of moral development, characterized by asking a lot of questions. Her little mouth can't keep up with all the questions her brain is sorting through. *Why does Mommy do that? I think I want to be like Mom, but does she really like doing that? Does it feel good? What if I don't like it? Maybe I will do it too, if she tells me why she does it.*

If something makes sense to her, she will embrace it, do it, and believe it. If it doesn't, she'll keep asking questions. I call this the counseling phase because there is a lot of dialogue. You get to counsel her as she figures out what she believes about life.

This phase of moral development can be downright exasperating for a mom! It is quite tempting to move quickly past the questions, thinking they're not important. (Did I mention that nurturing Truth is time-consuming?)

It helped me to remember that anytime the word *why* showed up, it was a spiritual question. This was particularly helpful when I could not for the life of me see the connection between the question and spiritual Truth. For example, I remember answering questions about why the grass smelled so strong when Bob was mowing. My daughter wondered if the grass felt pain. (Incidentally, the answer is, "Yes, it does." That lovely, grassy scent that wafts through your yard when it is freshly mowed is a vegetative distress signal.)

Here's what you have to remember. These questions are critical to rooting and nurturing Truth in your children. Answer them. All of them. Even the ones about the smell of grass.

And let God root you in His patience as you do. As you're growing in forbearance, your daughter will be sorting through your responses and lifestyle to decide what she really believes.

A brief conversation I had with a girl named Ruby shows the complex sorting of thoughts that help a child reject or embrace Truth. Read it in the case study on the next page. While they are still observing and copying us, it is with more discernment than before. By the end of their eleventh or twelfth year, they have a rather complex foundation for their belief system. The roots have been established, even if they have some growing to do.

At the end of your daughter's tween years, the basics of her belief system are generally in place. Not everything is accurate just yet, but that's why the last phase of moral development matters too.

A CASE STUDY:
RUBY

Ruby is a vibrant bundle of tween energy with a sweet, infectious giggle to match her bright smile. She and I were discussing the Ten Commandments, specifically God's instruction to rest on the Sabbath. She peppered me with a lot of questions.

What is the Sabbath? Well, is it on Sunday or Saturday? What does resting mean? Who is supposed to do it? Does that mean you can't cook or make your bed? Can you brush your teeth?

I answered them all one-by-one. Ruby finally fell quiet and sat still, but I could see that her brain was still processing thoughts.

"My mom and dad don't believe in Sabbath," she blurted out. "They might say that they do, but they don't rest on Sundays. Dad works on his papers and Mom cleans a lot."

THE COACHING PHASE (AGES 12+)
Adjusting Beliefs

By the age of twelve, your daughter is actively living out a set of moral values. This phase involves more reasoning as she allows what she believes to affect *her* behavior. At this point, you're now an observer of her rather than she being an observer of you. The questions in her head don't revolve around mom anymore, but herself. *How do I want to do this? Is there something I believe that will help me decide? Maybe I will do it, if it fits into what I believe.*

I call this the coaching phase because it's kind of like watching your daughter play in a sport. She determines the plays and makes the shots, but you're sitting on the sidelines waiting for her to take a break and rest on the bench beside you. There, you'll have the chance to influence what she believes by asking her why she chose certain behaviors or emotions.

Let me tell you about a mom whose coaching was fantastic when her middle school daughter, Laura, became extremely withdrawn:

Laura was suddenly unwilling to try new things. Chelsea, her mom, determined to find out if this was just normal developmental angst and insecurity, or some sticky feelings that needed to be addressed.

One quick after-school snack later, the pieces of the puzzle began to fit. Laura was being bullied at school and believed all the unkind things that were being said to her. Bad roots were being planted and were changing the emotional and behavioral patterns of this once vibrant and fearless little girl.

When Laura told Chelsea the name of the girl who was being so unkind, she knew something her daughter did not. The girl was suffering and in deep pain, because her parents were in the middle of a nasty divorce.

"I wanted to teach her to stand up for herself when untruthful things were said to her, but in the right way," reported Chelsea, who coached her daughter. Laura went to school with a simple assignment to gently, but truthfully, confront her bully. It took no small amount of coaxing and praying for her to gain the courage, but

Chelsea knew that recovering her daughter's personality and emotional health depended on this courageous Truth encounter.

"I know you're going through a hard time right now," Laura told the girl at school the next day. "Is there anything I can do to help you? I will do it, but you have to start being nice to me."

It changed everything. The bully wasn't such a mean girl after all, but a girl in deep pain and loneliness. Today the girls are good friends, and Laura's tenacious love for life has returned.

Not all efforts to coach our kids work quite so dramatically or quickly. Sometimes they won't internalize your coaching advice, and at other times they won't have the guts to apply it. The simple fact is that they aren't always going to get things right. Children—even young teens—are great observers, but terrible interpreters. They need our help adjusting what they believe so they can respond to life in Truth!

These are simple, accurate facts about how our children develop a belief system. But if you don't mind, I'd like to jump on my soapbox for a moment. It's time for me to unveil the thesis of this chapter and I'd like to do it with a little bit of *oomph*. Here we go:

NOW—DURING YOUR DAUGHTER'S TWEEN YEARS— IS THE MOST IMPORTANT TIME TO PLANT SEEDS OF TRUTH INTO HER HEART.

My friend George Barna, who invested several years of his life researching the religious beliefs and behaviors of Americans, says it this way:

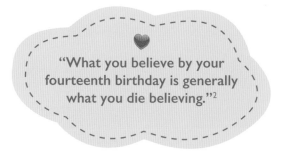

"What you believe by your fourteenth birthday is generally what you die believing."[2]

When I discovered this, I realized how critical it was for me to plant foundational Truth into my children during their tween years. It helped me gain the courage to send fear packing. I hope it'll do the same for you.

I know firsthand how hard it is to tell fear where the suitcases are stored. Here's a Bible verse I wore out while parenting my kids: ▼

 TRUTH NUGGET: "God has not given us a spirit of fear and timidity, but of power, love, and self-discipline." (2 Timothy 1:7)

We cannot parent out of a spirit of fear. It's not from God.

While I think many mothers embrace godly self-discipline to find the right timing and words for complex discussions, I also think some operate in fear when they avoid essential developmental conversations. Fear that they won't know what to say. Fear that it's too soon. Fear that it'll mess their daughter up. Fear that their daughter will be tempted by lies. Meditating on the fear often causes us to delay certain conversations far beyond reason. One mom actually said this in our focus groups: *"The best time to tell your daughter about sex is right before she is ready to do it. So, I think we should tell her on the night before her wedding."*

I believe *now*, while her heart is still afire with questions, is the time to plant Truth.

I'm not saying you should throw caution to the curb. Just the fear. You still need to use wisdom as you navigate difficult topics with age-appropriate care. It is a righteous desire *not* to want your daughter to have knowledge of good *and* evil. That is exactly what God was concerned about for Adam and Eve. He told them not to eat from the fruit of the tree to protect them. He didn't want firsthand experience to rob them of their innocence and, with it, bring terrible consequences.

As I mentioned earlier, only you can know when to introduce a topic to your daughter. If you decide your daughter is unable to developmentally grapple with a subject matter or has some special needs that would prevent her from mentally understanding something, you are choosing to delay conversations out of wisdom, not fear. But, if you are simply afraid of a topic or don't know how to approach it without robbing her of her innocence, those are not good reasons to avoid discussing something.

When we parent out of fear, we set our daughter up to listen to the voices that lie. Sadly, when it comes to Adam and Eve, they heard the one voice that could lie to them in the Garden of Eden. Satan had chosen a snake for the job. He now has many mouthpieces to speak his lies. In fact, it can be difficult for you and me to avoid them. Advertisements. Movies. Friends. Political systems. Even trusted leaders can sometimes be the source of lies. If we are not careful, our fear-driven silence becomes a megaphone for these voices to plant lies in our children.

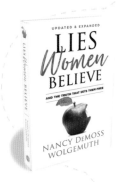

Are you struggling with fear as a mom? Rip up the lies you may be believing about your emotions by reading chapter 9 in *Lies Women Believe.*

Consider this: If your daughter is still copying you or in the phase of moral development where she questions you, what kind of impact could it have on her belief system if you learn to respond to your emotions with Truth?

In this chapter of *Lies Girls Believe*, your daughter is learning four ways that Eve cooperated with Satan.

Are you sure it's too soon to talk to your daughter about a certain topic? Or are you being deceived into thinking that it is too soon? The distinction matters so much because when you and I believe lies we cooperate with Satan. And helping him plant lies into my daughters is something I want to avoid.

We need to be alert and sensitive to the Spirit, to discern when it is necessary (and the right time) to step up and into difficult conversations. When we do, it is often easier than we thought it would be. After all, God only told Adam and Eve the Truth about the tree. He didn't mention the lie the snake would speak. I find that you can safely talk to your daughter about virtually any subject without introducing the lies that are not appropriate for her heart and mind. The lies are not what we emphasize. We want to direct our girls into the Truth.

But, if your daughter is not accurately hearing God's Truth, she cannot listen to it, dwell on it, believe it, or act on it. She cannot even recognize a lie when it begins to whisper into her ear, if she hasn't been told the Truth.

TALKING WITH GOD:

Use Proverbs 23:7 to write a prayer to God. Ask Him to give you clarity about what is in your daughter's heart. Let Him help you sort out what parts of her behavior are rooted in things that should not be in her heart. Write your honest petitions to God in the lines below.

As he thinks in his heart, so is he. (Proverbs 23:7 NKJV)

_____

_____

_____

_____

_____

TALKING WITH YOUR GIRL:

After your daughter reads chapter 2 in *Lies Girls Believe*, turn to page 33 and ask your daughter to explain to you the four ways that Eve cooperated with the snake. Ask her if she ever cooperates with lies in these ways.

Then, turn to page 29 where she wrote down what advice she would give Zoey about the temptation to disobey her parents. Discuss her ideas.

What's Grace Got to Do with It?

O ne thing I learned as I conducted the focus groups was this: we aren't very objective when it comes to our own daughters. This is undoubtedly something my husband will find great peace in seeing me admit to in writing. Here's how I finally came to understand something he has been trying to help me see for almost a quarter of a century.

At the beginning of each discussion, I asked mothers if they thought today's tween girls faced bigger problems than they did and if they thought today's girls were more prone to be in spiritual bondage to lies.

🍎 *80% of moms believed that today's tween girls are more prone to believe lies.*

But that didn't necessarily include *their* daughters.

🍎 *80% of moms were less concerned about their own daughters than other girls.*

The disparity seemed odd, so I probed a bit. I asked moms how their daughters reacted when they needed to be obedient or submit to rules. At first, they all made their daughters sound so lovely that I thought they might be the first generation of girls to completely conquer rebellion and bring peace to the world.

But then . . .

Each group of women generally had one brave mom who would step up to share a surprisingly complex case of disobedience. This was one of them.

A CASE STUDY: MOLLY

"The level of deception my daughter has stooped to in order to avoid submission has dumbfounded her dad and me," reported Janet.

Her daughter, Molly, is extremely intelligent and gets As and Bs on all her tests and quizzes. She scores in the 97th percentile on standardized tests. But, she doesn't like homework, and in second grade decided that she didn't need to do it anymore.

Her teacher, of course, didn't think this was a good idea and began sending notes concerning Molly's lack of obedience and submission. They never made it home.

Molly is currently in fifth grade. Janet and her husband have done everything they can think of to confront this issue and deal with their daughter's heart, but thus far, to no avail.

So, at the beginning of each school year, Janet meets with teachers to explain her daughter's problem with submission and to give teachers her cellphone number so they can call directly when Molly stops handing in homework.

Soon others would follow the lead of the brave mom, getting vulnerable about the struggles they faced when trying to get their daughters to respect authority and be obedient. They said things like:

🍎 *She does obey, but it is not from her heart. It is out of fear of consequences, and it is often delayed.*

🍎 *She demonstrates defiance, but only in small things like not putting on deodorant or failing to make her bed.*

🍎 *My daughter treats her father like a brother instead of a dad.*

🍎 *I'm just plain worn out by it.*

With their hearts opened to be honest, I took the next step. I wanted to not only inquire about the beliefs girls need to put to use in the here and now, but also those they will need in the future. So, I asked women what their daughters believed about the value of marriage and motherhood. While most mothers said that their girls wanted to be a wife and mom, 33 percent felt that their daughter seemed to think having a career or education was more important. This made them sad. Like me, they love being moms and can't imagine a better career.

After our discussion on obedience, submission, marriage, and motherhood, I took another stab at things, repeating my question about whether or not *their* daughters could be capable of believing lies. The results changed.

MOMS vs DAUGHTERS

I wanted to see if moms were accurately assessing their daughters' beliefs when it came to the topics of submission, obedience, marriage, and motherhood. I asked thirty-one of their daughters some questions to cross-check. The results showed some startling differences in their perspective. These differences may reveal an inner struggle in girls that moms are not adequately tuned in to.

67%
Moms who said their daughters value marriage and motherhood over having a career outside of the home

5%
Girls who said they value marriage and motherhood over having a career outside of the home

48%
Girls who felt a career outside of the home was more important than marriage and motherhood

ON FUTURE GOALS

76%
Moms who said their daughter struggles to obey

97%
Girls who admitted they struggle to obey

ON SUBMISSION

Only 56% of moms were still less concerned about their own daughters than other girls, after discussions on submission, obedience, marriage, and motherhood.

While that seemed more accurate, it still alarmed me. Consider with me that maybe a lot of us believe this lie at some point in our parenting journey.

▶ MOM LIE #3: ◀
"MY DAUGHTER IS NOT AT RISK LIKE OTHER GIRLS."

I get it. It was tempting to look at my girls when they were tweens and believe the lie that they couldn't possibly face the same temptations and challenges I encountered when I was their age. (There's some part of me that has frozen my children in time as innocent toddlers clad in footie pajamas!) Whatever *it* was, *it* wasn't coming into my home!

Some moms proudly inserted the word *sheltered* to describe their girls.

You may have sheltered them, protected them, filled them with Truth, and prayed for them diligently. That does not exempt them from being exposed to lies, believing them, and sinning. If it did, Eve would have never fallen prey.

The first woman lived in a world untouched by sin. No woman has ever lived a more sheltered life. There was no Netflix, social media, music, cliques, advertisements, or sin in the Garden of Eden. She walked and talked with a perfect Father who speaks only Truth. And yet, she listened to the first lying voice. And she believed the most cataclysmic lie ever told. *How is it that we believe our own daughters are not at risk?*

The truth is that your daughter is going to sin. All of us do (Romans 3:23). She is at risk, because humanity is at risk. For that reason, we must be prepared not only to plant Truth into her, but to nurture it with grace when she sins.

The story in the Garden models God's readiness to extend grace. He expected His children to sin, and He was prepared to respond to their fall with two things: comforting conversation and confrontation.

First, God comfortingly converses with them. He pursued them, and called out to them with a question: "Where are you?" For the record, He knew the answer to that. He is God. So, this question demonstrates the communal, interactive nature of godly discipline. Of course, Adam and Eve realized how utterly exposed they were, and they felt embarrassed. Ashamed. And God knew what they had done, why, and how they felt now. But He gave them the chance to verbalize it before rushing to explain the harsh realities of consequence. He had a conversation with them to help them understand their reaction and shame.

One of the important things about your daughter's behavior is not just what she has done, but why she has done it. The *why* is at the root of her belief system.

You may have a good idea why she was mean to her sibling today—she felt overwhelmed and jealous by the attention her little brother was getting at his birthday party. You may understand why she cheated on her reading test—she felt dumb and embarrassed by her recent diagnosis of dyslexia. You may think you know why she lied about having a horse—because she felt insecure when she was talking to new friends.

You may know it.

But she may not.

This is a good opportunity to remind her that Jesus is always there to help her, and will help you both sort out why she did something bad. In the pages of *Lies Girls Believe*, she is learning this definition of Truth.

TRUTH: *"agreement with a standard or original"*

Jesus is the standard and original source of what is true about us and about how we should act. He said: ▼

👑 **TRUTH NUGGET:** "I am the way, the truth, and the life." (John 14:6)

He is the definition of Truth. If you ask Him, He will reveal the Truth to you. He does this mostly through the written Word of God—the Bible! In fact, "the Word" is actually one of Jesus' names (John 1:14).

In the Bible, you'll find words that describe **WHO YOU ARE and HOW YOU SHOULD ACT**!

If your daughter is having a hard time understanding herself, she can ask Jesus for help. This is an essential part of walking in Truth. It is more time-consuming than simply sending her to her room or taking away her TV privileges, but it is also more lasting. It's true she may also have to lose privileges, but remember that consequences cannot be the only response to sin in her life. Every bad behavior is an opportunity to grow her understanding of right and wrong. Her behavior may have been sinful, but don't rush to consequence. Rush to find her lost heart, and to help her understand it.

🍎 *Let's talk about why you were unkind to your brother today.*

🍎 *What were you feeling when you cheated on this test?*

🍎 *Why did you think you needed to lie?*

Grace slows the consequences down just a bit to tend to the heart. Grace is an undeserved gift. God gave it to Adam and Eve. I'm asking you to wrap it up and give it to your daughter now and again in the form of a conversation. (Even if the dishes need to be done, you're running late to get your son to soccer practice, and you have an Etsy order to get in the mail today.)

Comforting your child with understanding is a vital part of nurturing her in Truth.

Later in the narrative, God provides even more comfort by offering Adam and Eve alternatives to their handmade fig-leaf clothing: He made fur coats for them. This is no small thing. We don't know which of God's beautiful, perfect creatures died that day, but something did (Genesis 3:21). We don't realize how costly a gift this was because we have grown up in a world acquainted with blood and death, but it was something God never wanted for His earth. Yet, for the love of His children, death came. Blood was shed, pointing to Christ, the Lamb of God, who would one day shed His blood so that we could be clothed in His righteousness.

I remember a time when one of my girls had spoken disrespectfully to me in front of others. My husband had no tolerance for that, and her punishment was to write the entire book of Proverbs out on college-ruled notebook paper. Bob explained to her that speaking back to authorities was not respectful and that many of the words she would write could help her gain wisdom.

Not gonna lie. It was painful to watch my tween baby spending countless evenings in her room seemingly emptying pens of ink as she wrote 9,921 words of Truth. (That's how many there are in the book of Proverbs. I checked.) A stack of tissues wetted with her tears grew taller as she worked.

At one point, Bob felt she had learned her lesson. (His clue was that she set about the work diligently, stopped playing on our emotions, and seemed to be having a better attitude.) So, he came in with comfort.

I watched them finish writing Proverbs as father and daughter. He wrote a verse. Then she wrote one. And so forth. He carried the consequence with her, and so comforted her.

Comforting your daughter when she has believed a lie and acted on it is not spoiling her. It includes getting to the root of why she sinned and preventing her from repeating it.

But it is spoiling her if you don't follow through with God's second act of grace: confrontation.

Second, God confronted them. Confrontation is not a form of punishment; it is discipleship. Punishment is dispensing consequences for sinful behaviors. Discipleship is confronting sinful behavior and heart attitudes, for the purpose of nurturing your child in the Truth. It may include consequences, but it is not limited to them—meaning, it does not end with them.

When God began the work of confronting Adam and Eve, He didn't start with the sad list of pain in childbirth, relationship problems, working hard, and so forth. He began with another question.

▶ What did you do?

As important as it is for your daughter to consider why she did what she did, it is also important that she knows she sinned. It is good for her to call it what it is: lying, cheating, bullying, stealing, sneaking onto social media, or watching a forbidden TV show. Ask her what she did.

The language of grace does not do away with the need for the vocabulary of sin. Of course, that's not a popular word in our post-Christian culture, and it isn't mentioned in many modern parenting books. But, I believe helping your daughter understand sin is imperative if you are going to help her walk in Truth.

Years ago, the famous psychiatrist Karl Menninger who was (as far as I know) not a self-proclaimed Christian, called for "a revival of sin." He wrote:

If a dozen people are in a lifeboat and one of them discovers a leak near where he is sitting, is there any doubt as to his responsibility? Not for having made the hole, or for finding it, but for attempting to repair it! To ignore it or to keep silent about it is almost equivalent to having made it!

Thus even in group situations and group actions, there is a degree of personal responsibility, either for doing or not doing or for declaring a position about it. The word "sin" involves these considerations, and upon this I base the usefulness of a revival of the concept, if not the word, sin.[2]

The story of sin in the Garden of Eden is a *hopeful* story. The assumption that there is sin—that there is right and wrong—brings with it the implication that decisions can be made. To this end, sin is a useful concept because your daughter can learn that she has a choice the next time she is faced with a sticky feeling, a lie, and the temptation to sin.

I think what our girls face today is probably a lot more confusing than what Adam and Eve experienced, though I cannot know for sure. At least Adam and Eve knew what was right and wrong (for God had told them clearly); so they knew when they had sinned. There was no uncertainty.

It's not as easy for some people to identify sin in a world governed by tolerance, acceptance, and hedonism. Erasing the concept of sin is confusing to our children. Without a strong compass for right and wrong, your daughter could become unsure of what to do the next time she is faced with a choice. But you can give her the grace-filled gift of confronting her sin.

I am not naturally a confrontational person, but I have learned that confrontation (when self-controlled and loving) is evidence of connection. It says, "I love you. I want to be in relationship with you, and you just put that at risk!" (Think about that the next time you have a fight with your husband or best friend or need to confront your child's sin.)

In addition, I have recently been convicted by the life of Eli, the priest. His sons were evil and unrestrained. The Bible says that Eli was punished not because they were bad, but because he did not confront their sin (1 Samuel 3:13).

I beg you, reject the lie that your daughter is not at risk like other girls.

This lie is deadly to our daughters because it disables our parental alarm system. It blinds us to the telltale signs of risk. Rather than exploring what lies may be under sticky feelings, we end up excusing and explaining them away as simply normal, developmental changes that all preadolescent children go through. Don't do that.

Arm yourself with the Truth that your daughter will sin, and be ready to rush in with grace to nurture the Truth with comforting conversation and unwavering confrontation.

♥ TALKING WITH GOD:

Use John 14:6 to write a prayer to God. Ask God to give you wisdom and confidence in discerning right and wrong so that you can teach it to your daughter. Bring Him any areas of confusion in your mind. Write your honest petitions to God in the lines below.

"I am the way and the truth and the life." (John 14:6)

_____

_____

_____

_____

_____

TALKING WITH YOUR GIRL:

After your daughter reads chapter 3 in *Lies Girls Believe*, turn to page 42 and discuss our definition of Truth. Make sure that she understands that Jesus, and His written Word, are the "standard or original" by which we judge our behaviors and moral choices.

Then, turn to page 44 where she has written the advice she would share with Zoey about feeling like the "worst person on the planet" and being "embarrassed." Discuss her ideas.

Lies Girls Believe
and the Truth That Sets Them Free

(Planting Seeds of Truth in
Your Daughter's Life)

Dannah

I t's time to uproot the lies tween girls believe and replace them with God's Truth. Many of the observations in this section about what girls believe will make perfect sense to you. Others may be surprising. But, everything has been carefully considered and validated with highly reliable evidence: the thoughts of tween girls.

1,531 girls took our survey!

These girls, ranging in age from seven to twelve, answered eighteen questions about how they think, feel, and believe. The vast majority considered themselves to be Christians.

- *51% were attending public school*

- *30% were being homeschooled*

- *16% were attending a private Christian school**

These girls' responses helped reveal twenty of the most common lies girls believe—lies that need to be replaced with Truth. Your daughter will come to know this section of her book as "The Truth Lab." Here's what she will read in her introduction to this section.

Sometimes when problems need to be solved, smart people spend time sorting through information in a laboratory, or lab. They're trying to find out what is true about something: the way our bodies heal, the secret to flying to the moon in a spaceship, or the way an animal responds to training. They are discovering and protecting truth for us, and for people who live in the future.

We need to discover and protect Truth to help us with our problems! There are so many lies confusing us that we need a place to organize and label the Truth. Otherwise, it might be lost forever. So, welcome to our Truth Lab!

* 3% of girls reported other methods of schooling such as private nonreligious school.

As your daughter learns to sort, store, and protect Truth, I'd like you to consider it a lab where you can plant seeds of Truth in her life. As you observe these seeds start to sprout, you can then nurture the young, tender roots that develop. You and I will work together to help her plant these seeds, fertilize them, and ultimately strengthen the roots of her belief system.

Each of these chapters will contain three sections.

PREPARING TO TALK:

At the beginning of each chapter, I'll present core results from the focus groups and survey. The focus groups with moms and the tween survey were my way of listening to you and your daughter. This book is my chance to respond. I hope that my use of Scripture to filter the information will get you revved up to plant Truth into your daughter on each specific topic.

TALKING WITH GOD:

Next, I will provide you with a prayer prompt. It will look similar to the ones you've already been using in this book, but will appear in the middle of the chapter instead of at the end. This way, you can pray for your girl before she starts digging into the subject at hand.

TALKING WITH YOUR GIRL:

This section of each chapter contains the material from your daughter's book right here in yours. You can read what she's reading, and be prepared to help her think through it. It also contains bonus content in the margins, exclusively for you.

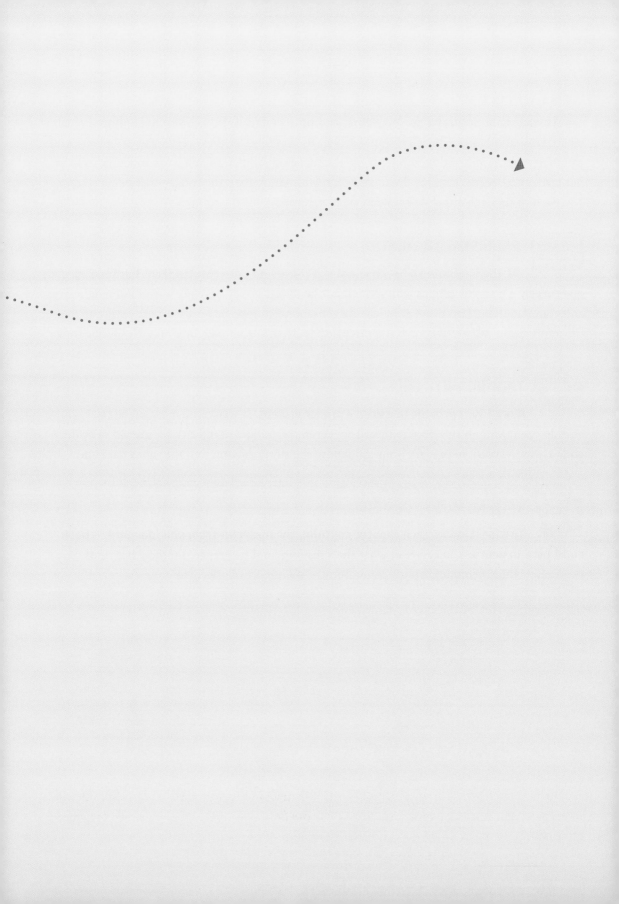

Truth and Lies about God

Tenure first topic your daughter will tackle in her Truth Lab is what she believes about God. These beliefs are foundational to what she thinks about everything else. As Nancy wrote in *Lies Women Believe*:

> *If we have wrong thinking about God, we will have wrong thinking about everything else. What we believe about God determines the way we live. If we believe things about Him that aren't true, we will eventually act on those lies and end up in various types of bondage.*[1]

Of course, this is true for us as mothers too. For me, presenting Truth about God to my daughters was once hindered by a lie I believed. Before I share it with you, I'd like to reveal something the moms in my focus groups communicated.

I asked moms this question: *"What kinds of lies are you most concerned about in your daughter's life?"* Here were the results:

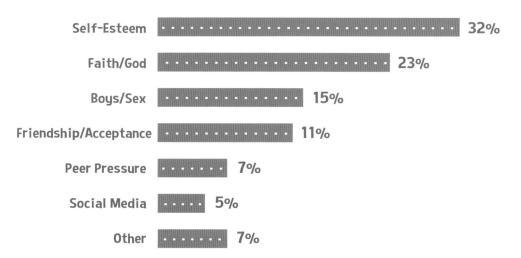

Self-Esteem	32%
Faith/God	23%
Boys/Sex	15%
Friendship/Acceptance	11%
Peer Pressure	7%
Social Media	5%
Other	7%

Each of these is important, and we'll cover them all in the next few chapters. But my first thought when I saw these results was this: *How can lies about faith and God not be the number one concern of Christian mothers?*

To explain why this was so emotional for me, I need to take you back a decade. My husband Bob and I were invited to a series of roundtable discussions to strategize and pray about how to reach and disciple tweens. Leaders from organizations such as AWANA, The Billy Graham Evangelistic Association, iShine, and Focus on the Family attended. Bob and I were included because of our interest in reaching tweens through events and resources. All of us shared a collective belief that the mass exodus of college-aged students from the church was a result of the lack of biblical training during the critical value-forming tween years.

Pollster George Barna, who was part of our group, warned that only about one-third of preteens in the United States considered themselves to be Christians, which would predict a stronger departure from the church in coming years.[2] He went on to reveal specific lies preteens believed at the time including:

- *80% believed the Bible, the Book of Mormon, [and] the Koran were the same*

- *68% believed you could earn your salvation*

- *56% believed Jesus may have sinned while He was on earth*

- *Only 36% believed the Bible to be accurate*

- *Only 32% believed Jesus had resurrected from the dead*[3]

Then Barna said the words that would completely undo me.

> "I beg you . . . invest the bulk of your resources—time, money, prayers—into children."[4]
>
> GEORGE BARNA

Tears of conviction and repentance filled my eyes. You see, I was devoting my time, money, and prayers into children, and it was what I loved doing. However, the emotion I often felt when I talked about my work was best described as embarrassment. (Did you just identify a sticky feeling in my story?)

I didn't realize it until that day, but I'd assumed my work was not as important as that of Christian authors and speakers who ministered to adult women. I believed the lie that investing into the faith of children wasn't quite as valuable.

I lived this belief out as a mother, too. Ultimately, we prove what we believe by how we act. At the time, I was working to plant biblical Truth into my children. But I *felt* like the hours I invested into their academics, hobbies, health, and friendships were considerably more strategic than the time I invested into their faith.

Let me be honest: the Christian world feeds this lie. It often makes much of the books I release for teens and women, but the radio interviews, marketing budgets, and blogger reviews for the books I write for younger girls are fewer and further between. Maybe you have noticed the same dynamic in your church. The children's ministry budgets and the amount of time devoted to kids on the main platform are often so small.

That just doesn't make sense! According to a survey conducted by the International Bible Society, 83 percent of Americans make their commitment to follow Christ between the ages of four and fourteen.[5] Based on this alone, we should be providing meaty spiritual content to children.

But we have a much more sinister motivator right now: sadly, Barna's predictions from over a decade ago have come true. We are witness to more children growing up to leave the church than ever before. As I write this, the percentage of today's emerging adults that identify as atheist is double that of the rest of the U.S. adult population.[6]

. . . . ATHEISM BY GENERATION[7] . . . .

13% Gen Z	7% Millennials	6% Gen X	5% Boomers	6% Elders

The faith of Generation Z—that's anyone born between 1999–2015—is in crisis. They're the first truly "post-Christian" generation, born "in a time of growing religious apathy."[8] A Biola University survey recently revealed that 70 percent in this age group express "persistent, measurable doubts that what the Bible says about Jesus is true. And these are 'cream of the crop' youth group kids."[9]

As moms, lies about faith and God should be our number one concern. For me, it was, but my work was hobbled by untruth that resided deep within my spirit. I had to overcome the lie that ministering to children—including my own—wasn't as important as other work in the Kingdom. How did I do that? I found this Truth to contradict my emotions and the voices around me. ▼

 TRUTH NUGGET: "Jesus said, 'Let the children come to me. Don't stop them! For the Kingdom of Heaven belongs to those who are like these children.'" (Matthew 19:14)

Jesus spoke these words for people like me—the ones believing the lie that the spiritual lives of children are less important than that of adults. Anything Jesus says trumps the other voices in my head. I've chosen to align myself with this Truth and do everything I can to bring the hearts of children as close to Him as possible, starting with my own three kids, Robby, Lexi, and Autumn.

When I initially witnessed mothers in our focus groups prioritizing "lies about self-esteem" over "lies about God," I was heartbroken. Then, I remembered my own battle for Truth and the way He helped me win it. Remembering this victory made me feel hopeful.

Be honest with yourself as you consider how effectively you are planting Truth about God into your daughter. Don't be afraid to assault any lies that hinder you. Press into hope.

TALKING WITH GOD:

Use Matthew 19:14 to write a prayer to God. Remind yourself that planting seeds of Truth into your daughter is some of the most important kingdom work you'll ever do. Ask God to check your heart to see if there's resistance to or apathy about talking to your daughter about Him. Write your honest petitions to God in the lines below.

Jesus said, "Let the children come to me. Don't stop them! For the Kingdom of Heaven belongs to those who are like these children." (Matthew 19:14)

_____

_____

_____

_____

TALKING WITH YOUR GIRL:

Now that you've prayed, invite your daughter to read chapter 4 in her book while you review the same content right here in your book. I've written a few notes for you in the margins. As you read, you may want to add your own notes to prompt you when it's time to discuss this chapter with your girl.

Truth and Lies about God

CHAPTER 4

I'm glad that whole **thing** with the app is over. I do feel better since you helped me think about the Truth. But I have a question: is God mad at me? **I know He loves me . . .** it feels like He may be far away because of what I did. Does He love me **even** when I do something bad?

Zoey is in the right place for us to dig into the Bible for the Truth that sets all of us girls free. She wonders if God loves her even after she sins. Have you ever wondered that? Truth #1 is good news for all of us.

TRUTH #1 God loves you *all the time*, no matter what!

NOTES FOR MOM

For the next few chapters, I'm embedding the entire chapter of your daughter's book here for you to review. The margin will contain interesting tidbits from our focus groups and survey. I hope these empower and direct you as you point your girl toward Truth.

Remember, this space is also for you to write notes in!

NOTES FOR MOM

About Truth #1:

After each survey question, we gave girls a chance to sound off on the topic. The comments for this one revealed an alarming disconnect. The majority of the girls knew God loved them, but their responses revealed a lack of confidence in His love when they sinned. They wrote things like this:

💜 *I sometimes think that God doesn't love me when my behavior is bad to my parents or friends.*

💜 *Sometimes when I disobey it's hard to believe He loves me.*

💜 *God might not feel the same way about me when I act or talk or dress [a certain way].*

💜 *I feel like He's not there when I'm not good enough.*

Anytime we say one thing but *feel* another, there's a lie that needs to be addressed.

▶ 92% of girls are sure God loves them.

I t's great that so many girls believe God loves them, but the Truth is even better. God loves 100% of humans **all the time**, no matter what. And that includes you!

God loves you. A lot!

The Bible tells us this Truth over and over. One of my favorite verses is Isaiah 43:4, which includes the simple words: "I love you."

Even so, I discovered that this Truth is hard for some girls to believe when they have done something bad, like disobey their parents or cheat on a test.

Sometimes their feelings tell them a lie about God's love.

▶ **LIE: "GOD ONLY LOVES ME WHEN I'M GOOD."** ◀

Have you ever believed that lie? I think most of us have at some point in our lives. Sin makes it difficult to **feel** God's love even though it is still there. Trying to feel connected to God after we sin can be like trying to download a song or listen to an episode of *Adventures in Odyssey* when you don't have good Wi-Fi. The connection is there, but something is interfering with it.[10]

Sin makes it hard for us to connect clearly to God. (I'm going to explain more about that in another chapter.) **But God is still there. And He still loves you!**

Yes, He feels sad when you sin and sometimes there are consequences, but that doesn't mean He doesn't love you. Let's see what our Truth Lab is storing up from God's Word. ▼

👑 **TRUTH NUGGET:** "But God showed his great love for us by sending Christ to die for us while we were still sinners." (Romans 5:8)

God is not surprised by your sin. He knows **EVERYTHING**. No matter what you have done or how much you have messed up, God still loves you and will forgive you.

I understood this better after I became a mother. Once when my son was little, he asked for water. He then promised he had **not** played with the lit candle in the other room. **That seemed like a funny thing to say!** (And, by that time, I could smell smoke.) Thankfully, only the edge of a blanket had caught on fire, and I was able to put it out quickly. You know what? Even as I rescued him from his own mistake, I did not love him any less. In fact, I put that fire out **because of love**. I wanted to keep him safe.

How much more does God, in all of His perfection, love you? He loves you when you behave well **and** when you behave badly.

Nancy

I've asked Dannah to start by looking at the lies girls believe about God. Nothing is more important than this. If you believe things about God that are not true, you will end up believing lots of other things that are not true.

NOTES FOR MOM

Conversation Tip for Truth #1:

The more your daughter opens up to you, the more you can help her. Vulnerability breeds vulnerability. Consider using your conversation time to share with her an instance when you sinned, and how it made you question God's love. Be sure to tell her how you discovered that God loves you *all the time*, no matter what.

Also, begin to be intentional about modeling this kind of unconditional love. Does your daughter see that you love her *all the time*, no matter what? Living out this Truth can drive it home.

"There is nothing we can do to make God love us more. . . . there is nothing we can do to make God love us less."

—Philip Yancey[11]

NOTES FOR MOM

About Truth #2:

Nancy first addressed this one in *Lies Women Believe*. If she wrote about it for adult women, your daughter probably isn't going to out-grow it naturally. Today she might need good grades or a best friend, but tomorrow it will be a husband or a bigger house. These things are wonderful gifts from Him, but they cannot be our first desire. Let's uproot the lie that anything other than God can truly satisfy.

Make a note in the margin below about what your daughter might try to use to satisfy her desires. Fill in this sentence: "She thinks her life would be better if _____

_____

_____

_____

_____

_____

_____."

TRUTH #2 God is all you need!

G od is all you need, because He loves you and will supply anything else you really need. Eve didn't believe this wonderful Truth. Instead, she believed: **My life would be better if I just had a bite of that fruit!**

Way back then, she faced a lie that some girls still believe.

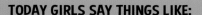

▶ **LIE: "GOD IS NOT ENOUGH."** ◀

TODAY GIRLS SAY THINGS LIKE:

🍎 "My life would be better if I had STRAIGHT As!"

🍎 "My life would be better if I had a PET!"

🍎 "My life would be better if I had a FRIEND!"

Almost every girl has believed that last lie. When I talked to girls, they said things like, **"The most important part of church is good friends."** Or, **"The reason we picked my church is that I have friends there."** What they were saying is: **"God is not enough. I need a friend too."**

My friends help me grow closer to God, and to make good choices. I hope yours do, too. But our friends shouldn't be more important than God. Check out this Truth Lab Bible verse. ▼

 TRUTH NUGGET: "God who takes care of me will supply all your needs from his glorious riches . . ." (Philippians 4:19)

There is nothing wrong with having friends, a great family vacation, or a cute pair of jeans. Sometimes they **are** a great addition to our lives. But none of

NOTES FOR MOM

these things are as good or as useful as God. He is the one who gives us everything—our friendships, our brains, the pets we love, the money we use to buy clothes, and more. Only He can ever be enough.

My real live friend, 10-year-old Jenna Jones, has grown up in Germany where her parents are missionaries. Here's how she learned that Truth.

Jenna Jones, Berlin, Germany

"For the very first time ever I was going to live in America for a year. I was so scared. I thought to myself, 'I don't want to go. I won't have any friends.'"

Her family arrived in the United States during summer break, and Jenna **decided** to try to be happy even without friends. As weeks went by, she experienced a better friendship with Jesus. She had no idea what a good friend He could be. She began to believe she could do anything, if God was with her. That included going to a new school with no friends.

Then came the first day of school. The morning was hard, as friends greeted each other and caught up. All morning, she tried to concentrate on her schoolwork and kept quietly asking God for help. She couldn't believe it, but she felt okay.

Little did she know, God had a gift waiting.

"At recess, I made a lot of friends when we played soccer together."

She believes God gave her those friends. Sometimes He is capable of making friends in ways that we could never dream.

God wants to be the most important person in your life. And—pay close attention to this—He wants you to know that you can be content and even happy if He chooses not to give you something you want. Jenna was content through her summer and that first morning at school even though she didn't have any friends yet. He wants you to know the Truth that He alone is **enough**.

GOD + YOU = ENOUGH!

Conversation Tip for Truth #2:

Friendship *does* matter. It *is* important. The Bible says that when we walk with wise friends, we grow wise. So, the problem isn't that your daughter has a desire for friends, it's that she may have a *lack* of desire to pursue a relationship with the most important friend: Jesus.

Start your conversation by talking about how even best friends sometimes let us down. (Realistic expectations help girls respond better to friendship drama.) Then, tell your daughter how you have experienced an authentic relationship with Christ, and encourage her that there is no better friend than Him because He never lets us down.

About Truth #3:

One girl who took our survey wasn't sure whether she was a Christian or not. When she was asked to articulate what it means, she became confused. The good news is that she went directly to her mom for advice. Right then and there, they prayed and she was adopted into God's family!

Does your daughter have an accurate understanding of what it means to become a Christian? I'm praying hard about this one, and can't wait to hear how God uses this conversation.

Big Question:

If someone were to ask you about your daughter's relationship with Christ, would you know enough to give an accurate answer?

TRUTH #3 You are a Christian if you believe in Jesus and receive Him as your Savior.

When I looked at the answers 1,531 girls gave me for my questions about Truth and lies, I saw something sad.

22% percent of girls who claim to be a Christian do not understand how to become one.

THESE GIRLS SAID THINGS LIKE:

- I am a Christian because I go to church.
- I am a Christian because my mom and dad are Christians.
- I am a Christian because I have always been one.

Uh-oh! We have a big problem. There is a lie lurking, and it's hiding behind a lot of different things.

▶ LIE: "I AM A CHRISTIAN BECAUSE _____." ◀

Going to church can be great, but it does not make you a Christian. Having parents who are Christians is awesome, but that does not make you a Christian either. And, no one has "always been one."

HOW DO YOU BECOME A CHRISTIAN?

I'm glad you asked. God loves us so much He sent His Son Jesus to die on the cross for us. The Bible says it this way: ▼

 TRUTH NUGGET: "For this is how God loved the world: He gave his one and only Son, so that everyone who believes in him will not perish but will have eternal life." (John 3:16)

Why did Jesus die for us? He died because of our sin.

We have already talked about sin, but let's review. When we disobey God or choose to do wrong, we sin. Things like being mean, lying, or cheating are examples of sin. The Bible says that every single human who ever walked the earth has sinned. That includes you and me.

Sin separates us from God. And the Bible says the punishment for sin is death. **BUT GOD LOVES US**, so He sent His Son Jesus to die on a cross. The great news is that Jesus didn't stay dead. He came back to life with the power to forgive our sins. And, He offers us the free gift of His salvation.

SIN SEPARATES YOU FROM GOD.

NOTES FOR MOM

Conversation Tip for Truth #3:

The content in your daughter's book includes everything you need to help her understand what it means to follow Jesus. Read through it conversationally and ask her the questions I've written including:

💜 *"Why did Jesus die for us?"*

💜 *"What does sin do?"*

💜 *"Do you believe in Jesus?"*

💜 *"Are you ready to receive Jesus as your Savior?"*

If your daughter demonstrates conviction and understanding as you talk about these questions, ask the Spirit to help you discern whether she is ready to turn her life over to Christ. The prayer printed in her book may be helpful as a guide. Remember, though, that the goal is not to get her to "pray a prayer," but to genuinely respond to the work of the Spirit in her life, in repentance and faith.

If your daughter has already trusted Christ as her Savior, use this time to celebrate that with her, and talk about what it means to continue growing in her relationship with Him.

NOTES FOR MOM

Go ahead and jot out some thoughts to help you remember what you want to say to your girl right here.

I don't know about you, but I've never gotten a free gift without having to reach out to accept it. You accept God's free gift of salvation by **believing** in Jesus and **receiving** Him as your Savior.

TO **BELIEVE** IN JESUS MEANS:

- 💜 to trust Jesus
- 💜 to know Jesus is God's Son
- 💜 to know Jesus saves you from your sin
- 💜 to be willing to give Jesus control of your life

DO YOU BELIEVE IN JESUS?

If so, you are ready to **receive** Jesus as your Savior, which means you ask Jesus to live inside of you and be in charge of your life. Romans 10:9 reads, "If you openly declare that Jesus is Lord and believe in your heart that God raised him from the dead, you will be saved."

Have you ever received Jesus by asking Him to forgive you of your sins? If not, would you pray this prayer now?

Dear Lord, I admit to you that I am a sinner. I thank you for sending Jesus to die on the cross for my sins. I ask you to forgive me of my sins. I invite you to come into my life to be my Lord. Thank you for saving me. In Jesus' Name, Amen.

**Did you just pray that prayer for the first time?
If so, write the date below.**

The date I became a Christian:

Congratulations! Now, be sure to tell someone like your mom or your pastor. They're going to be so excited!

I hope the person you tell is also a Christian and can help you grow. Remember, you've just given Jesus control of your life. This mean's you'll obey Him and do what He asks you to do. Praying that prayer is just the first step in being a Christian. Now, your life needs to be lived as if you have changed. Ask this person to help you know how to grow.

NOTES FOR MOM

**TALKING WITH
YOUR GIRL:**

**After your daughter
reads chapter 4** in
Lies Girls Believe, ask her
to turn to page 60 so you
can discuss her lab work.
This page is important and
should be approached with
care and wisdom. You're
planting Truth, discover-
ing where lies may need
uprooting, and nurturing
the roots of Truth, which
already exist.

NOTES FOR MOM

About Your Daughter's Lab Work:

At the end of each chapter in her book, your daughter will have some lab work to do. It gives you both a chance to identify any lies she is believing and to talk about them.

Ask her if she put an X beside any of the lies, signifying that she might believe it. Explore your daughter's heart with questions.

"Why did you put an X by that lie?"

"Do you remember a time when you first started to believe it?"

"Was there something in the chapter that made you feel like this was a lie you wanted to tackle in your life?"

Next, ask her if she drew any circles around key Truths. Prompt her with questions.

"That's a neat Truth to circle, why did you pick it?"

"Is there a way that I can help you believe that Truth?"

If your daughter doesn't seem to want to talk, that's okay. Be patient with her and model transparency.

End your conversation by having her share her prayer to God, Bible verse, or practical idea. If she hasn't yet completed this part of the

---

At the end of each chapter, I'll remind you of the topics we examined in the Truth Lab. Then, you get to help Zoey by giving her some advice. Finally, you get to answer some questions that help **you** tell yourself Truth.

PUT ON YOUR LAB COAT

THE LIE	THE TRUTH
God only loves me when I am good.	• **God loves you all the time, every day.** (Isaiah 43:4) • **God loves you even though you sin.** (Romans 5:8)
God is not enough.	• **God is all you need.** (Psalm 23:1) • **God provides all your needs.** (Philippians 4:19) • **Jesus wants to be your best friend.** (John 15:15)
I am a Christian because _____.	• **You become a Christian when you believe Jesus is the Son of God who died for your sins . . .** (John 3:16) • **. . . and you ask Him to live inside you and be in charge of your life.** (Romans 10:9)

TRUTH LAB REVIEW

TELLING MYSELF THE TRUTH
It's your turn to be the author!

💜 Have you believed any of these lies about God? Put an X on top of any of **THE LIES** in this chapter that you have believed.

💜 What Truth do you need to think about **all the time**, EVERY DAY? Look at **THE TRUTH** we dug up together. Now circle what seems important for you personally to dwell on.

💜 Next, begin to think about it **all the time**, EVERY DAY. You can start by writing a prayer to God, a helpful Bible verse, or some ideas you don't want to forget in the space below.

Helping Zoey Believe Truth
It's time to give Zoey some advice!

Zoey feels far away from God because she lied to her parents. Based on what you learned in this chapter, is God really as far away as Zoey feels He is? What can she do to feel closer to her parents?

? ? ?

NOTES FOR MOM

lab work, offer to help her. Her age and maturity level will have a lot to do with how much assistance, if any, she needs.

About Helping Zoey:

The purpose of this lab work is to help your daughter's mind, heart, and mouth develop the skill of speaking Truth to a friend.

Don't be quick to criticize if she offers bad advice, or none at all. Instead, ask her questions to draw out a strong answer.

"What made you give Zoey that advice?"

"Is there a Bible verse you can think of that supports your idea?"

"A Bible verse that just came to my mind is _____. How can we apply that Truth to Zoey's circumstances?"

This task is complex. Expect her answers to be brief and possibly even incomplete, but know that she is learning the vital skill of becoming a Truth-speaking friend.

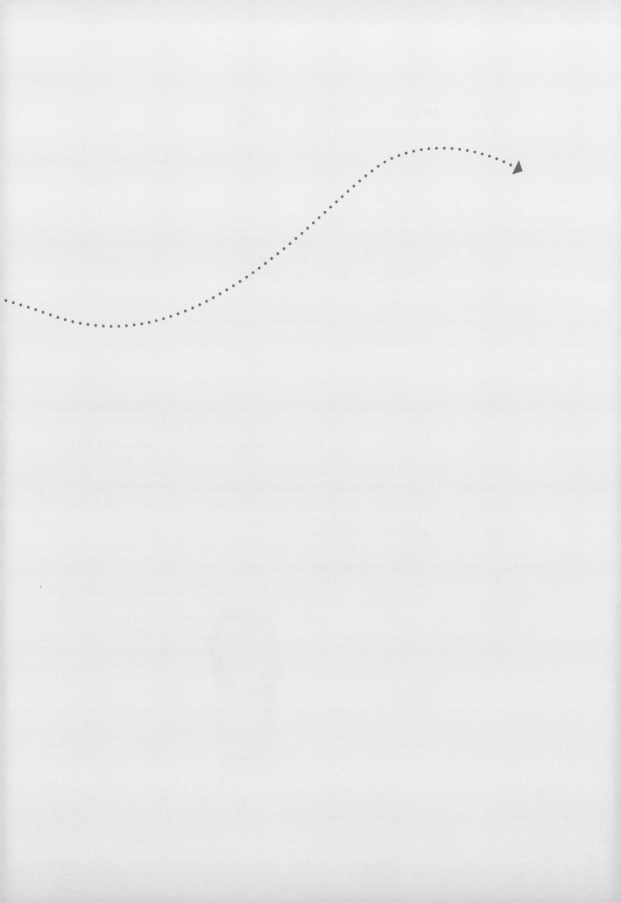

Truth and Lies about Myself

L̲ast night one of my now-grown baby girls—I still call them that—sat on the edge of my bed and we tried to hash out a problem. She told me what was troubling her and then asked, "What should I do?"

That's when it hit me! The mind-numbing sense of comatose—which I mentioned in chapter 1—showed up to make me shut up. My young adult daughter was giving me the gift of an invitation to be her wise counsel, and I was wordless.

I prayed, asking God to loosen my lips. He was faithful to bring the right words. What a sweet time I had with my daughter. The battle was easy for me this time because I have fought it many times and learned to use Truth and prayer to combat the numbness.

Many moms experience this same sense of feeling disabled when their daughter needs advice or discipline. In the focus groups, several women used the word *comatose* to describe the strange sensation that overtakes us. I asked them to try to discern what caused it.

I think many of us are afraid of being legalistic . . . so we bend in places we shouldn't. We fear we might cause her to believe unhealthy things about herself.

Rebellion. Sometimes it seems as if everything is a battle and I fear rebellion. If she doesn't feel affirmed, she might reject my advice.

Knowing how to articulate Truth. Feeling a lack of confidence in how to parent. Fearing I'll mess it up, and wound her sense of self.

It's fear based. I don't want to alienate her, ruin our relationship, or destroy her self-esteem.

Do you see the common denominator? Fear. (Didn't we send that emotion packing way back in chapter 2?) But this fear was attached to something very specific. Though each woman's fear manifested differently, it was often rooted in the sense that a mom might disrupt her daughter's self-confidence or self-esteem.

When I first began to experience this, it didn't take long for me to realize that I feared embarrassing my girls or hurting their feelings with my words. Even when I knew *what* to say, I didn't know *how* to say it without possibly making a dent in their self-confidence. After all, there were a host of other forces trying to take a swipe at them, and I didn't want to be another. From mean girls to beauty product advertising, it seemed life was one great big self-esteem land mine after another.

I took my fear to God and asked Him to give me clarity. That's when I detected a lie in my belief system:

The most important thing about raising my girls is protecting their self-esteem.

After some research and wise counsel, I came to embrace this Truth:

**The most important thing about raising girls is not
what they feel about themselves, but what God says.**

That's when I jumped off the self-esteem bandwagon.

Maybe you have never experienced the comatose feeling, but it's highly likely that you've believed your daughter's self-esteem is an utmost priority. After all, it was the number one priority of moms who attended my focus groups. But is that really what's most important?

In opposition to this mentality, God's Word warns us not to think too highly of ourselves (Romans 12:3). We aren't supposed to seek our own good, but the good of others (1 Corinthians 10:24). When we boast, we're encouraged to brag about our weaknesses so Christ's strength can shine through us (2 Corinthians 11:30). We're to submit to others (Hebrews 13:17), be humble towards others (1 Peter 5:5–7), and clothe ourselves in humility (Colossians 3:12). And that's just a handful of the many verses that encourage us to hold ourselves in low esteem compared to others and Christ. What have you done lately to teach your daughter these Truths?

I'm not saying you should ignore unhealthy, low self-worth if it manifests in your daughter. Sometimes a child *does* need help understanding their value and repairing the damage done by the world. The Bible says we should love our neighbor as ourselves (Matthew 22:39). This presupposes a certain sense of self-care, respect, and love. I simply think we've taken it too far.

Second Timothy 3 warns that love of self is the root of sin. (It's a root you don't want growing in your daughter's heart.) The same passage warns that love of self will be a sign of the end times and will bring with it many terrible sins. ▼

 TRUTH NUGGET: "You should know this, Timothy, that in the last days there will be very difficult times. For people will love only themselves and their money. They will be boastful and proud, scoffing at God, disobedient to their parents, and ungrateful. They will consider nothing sacred. They will be unloving and unforgiving; they will slander others and have no self-control. They will be cruel and hate what is good. They will betray their friends, be reckless, be puffed up with pride, and love pleasure rather than God." (2 Timothy 3:1–4)

Now, here's something I find especially alarming.

Many of the moms I spoke with who stated that self-esteem was the number one concern they had for their daughter, were witness to an ironic twist. Their girls, who were struggling with low self-esteem, often displayed a strong sense of self-entitlement.

These moms were frustrated with their daughters' lack of submission, unkindness towards others, disrespect for authority, and craving for material things. Do you see those things represented in the Bible verse above? The verse above seems to warn us that when the love of self becomes a preeminent concern, qualities like disobedience, ungratefulness, loving pleasure, and betrayal of friends will mark a person's life.

The girls who were struggling with low *self-esteem*, often displayed a strong sense of *self-entitlement*.

It's not that God doesn't care how your daughter feels about herself. If the Bible is rich with anything, it is the Truth that in God's eyes we have incredible worth. Ephesians 1 is a favorite spot for me to be reminded of what God thinks of my girls and me. It declares that we are chosen, blessed with every spiritual blessing, loved, made holy, adopted, forgiven, united with Christ, heirs of Christ, and more. And that's what we can glean in just one out of 1,189 chapters in the Bible.

What your daughter believes about herself must be rooted in what God says, not what she feels. Keep encouraging her to believe His Word and, in time, she will feel loved, accepted, and forgiven. The feelings of low self-esteem cannot enter into a heart that is sure of what it means to be in Christ.

Your daughter does not need greater self-esteem. She needs greater God-esteem. If she understands who God is, she will be aware of her value while not making too much of herself.

TALKING WITH GOD:

Use 2 Timothy 3:1–4 to examine your heart and your daughter's life. Is self-love creating sinful tendencies in either of you? Circle the things on this list that manifest in your life and/or in your daughter's life. Ask God what He would have you do about it. Write your confessions and petitions to God on the next page.

> *You should know this, Timothy, that in the last days there will be very difficult times. For people will love only themselves and their money. They will be boastful and proud, scoffing at God, disobedient to their parents, and ungrateful. They will consider nothing sacred. They will be unloving and unforgiving; they will slander others and have no self-control. They will be cruel and hate what is good. They will betray their friends, be reckless, be puffed up with pride, and love pleasure rather than God. (2 Timothy 3:1–4)*

_____

_____

_____

_____

_____

_____

TALKING WITH YOUR GIRL:

Now that you've prayed, invite your daughter to read chapter 5 in her book while you review the same content here in your book. I've written a few notes for you in the margins. You might want to add your own notes to prompt you when it's time to discuss this chapter with your girl.

Lies about Myself

CHAPTER
5

A new girl moved into our neighborhood this week. Her name is Isabella and her long legs make her run fast. So, of course, she got picked first for kickball today. Who got picked *last*? ME! The girl with the **SHORT** legs. **Again!!!**

Zoey isn't alone! When it comes to kickball, I remember being picked last too—over and over again. It felt really bad. But when I discovered the Truth, it helped a lot. I believe it'll help you too.

NOTES FOR MOM

Doodle your heart out if you have something you want to tell your daughter about lies she believes about herself.

NOTES FOR MOM

About Truth #4:

One characteristic that reveals a lie is what the Bible calls double-mindedness. A person who is double-minded has thoughts and actions that vacillate and waiver. A person like this is unstable (James 1:8).

For example, if a girl is disre-spectful toward her teachers but has an extreme lack of confidence when interacting with her peers, she is unsta-ble. The way she relates to others will be unreliable.

Double-mindedness was apparent to me when the moms named their daugh-ter's self-esteem as the top priority in this project, but also included entitlement as a big concern. They reported things like this:

💜 *Girls today have the right to question authority, but don't have the confi-dence to speak up in front of their peers.*

💜 *There is more targeted advertising. Media giants target tween girls. Now our daughters feel they are not beautiful, but demand makeup, food, clothing that they think they legitimately need.*

💜 *My daughter doesn't have the confidence to raise her hand to answer a question in class. At the same time, she treats her dad more like a brother and does not respect him.*

TRUTH #4 God chose you!

You are the work of THE Master Artist, God. The Bible says that He **knit** you together, which means He carefully planned and crafted you. Have **you** ever done any knitting? It requires **MATH**! It's careful and precise. If you don't count correctly, your knitting will turn into a mess. The stitches have to be accurate, or the appearance will be super sloppy!

Here's the point: God didn't just randomly throw a bunch of stuff together and say, "Uh oh! Will you look at that? I guess I made an Emma!" (Or a Zaani or a Chloe.) Nope! He carefully planned and made you. Every ability you have was planned by God.

Even so, there might be days when you don't feel so good about yourself. It happens.

SOMETIMES, GIRLS HAVE THOUGHTS LIKE THESE:

🍎 **I'm not smart enough.**   🍎 **I'm not strong enough.**

🍎 **I'm not fast enough.**   🍎 **I'm not funny enough.**

🍎 **Or, fill in the blank: I'm not** _____ **enough.**

These thoughts happen when we compare ourselves to other people, and listen to the opinions of others. One way we see the opinion of others is when they choose us . . . or when they don't.

It **hurts** not to be chosen. I remember how I felt when it happened to me: rejected, embarrassed, and judged.

My thoughts about it grew into a big, fat lie.

▶ LIE: "I'M NOT GOOD ENOUGH." ◀

This lie comes with some serious "sticky" feeling super glue. When we start to believe this lie, it's about more than our kickball skills or our math grade. It feels like we wear an all-out-nasty label that defines us.

Guess what!? Jesus understands. He also had people judging Him, overlooking Him, rejecting Him, and "not choosing" Him! The Bible says Jesus understood the weaknesses humans face, and He even had the same temptations as you and me. Since we are tempted to believe we are not good enough, it is likely that He was too. Though we don't know exactly how, Isaiah 53:2 tells us that He wasn't especially good-looking. He had at least this **one** thing about Him that was "less than" others around Him.

I'm pretty sure He was aware of this, **BUT** . . . the Bible tells us He never sinned. That means He never believed any lies! So, why didn't Jesus ever believe the lie that He wasn't good enough?

Well, 1 Peter 2:4 tells us that "Christ . . . was rejected by people, but he was chosen by God for great honor." **JESUS** was rejected by men. People said things about Him that were not good, **but He didn't listen to those opinions. Instead, He chose to believe what God the Father said about Him**. That was the only opinion that mattered to Him, and the one He used to decide what to believe about Himself.

Let's look at what God says about YOU to help you know what to believe about yourself. ▼

 TRUTH NUGGET: "Even before he made the world, God loved us and chose us in Christ to be holy and without fault in his eyes." (Ephesians 1:4)

Your confidence is always going to nose-dive if you compare yourself to others, and listen to their opinion of you. Stop obsessing about who did not choose you! Instead, **focus on the One who has chosen you!**

START **LISTENING** TO
AND **BELIEVING**
GOD'S OPINION ABOUT **YOU.**

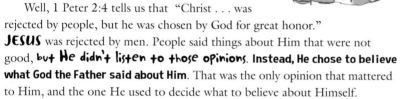

▶ He knows the Truth.
And the Truth is, God chose you,
and He'd choose you every time.

NOTES FOR MOM

Which is it? Does your daughter feel bad about herself? Or does she feel entitled?

Rather than confronting your daughter about entitlement, I've chosen first to introduce her to the Truth that she has great worth.

Conversation Tip for Truth #4:

The world is full of negative thoughts for us to believe. Tell your daughter about a time when someone said unkind things about you, or you thought something negative over and over again. Ask your daughter if there is anything someone has said to her lately that makes her feel bad about herself. Research suggests that children tend to hide painful communication, rather than tell a parent who can help them navigate what is true.

Big Question:

How can your daughter choose to believe what God the Father says about her if she isn't regularly reading what He has written about her in the Bible?

NOTES FOR MOM

About Truth #5:

What do *you* believe about beauty?

One mom who attended our focus group in Ohio said,

"I've gained five pounds in the past few months. I'm getting older and it's upsetting to me. It's so sad to me that as an adult I'm still worried about what people think. I thought I would grow out of it, and to realize I AM THE ONE who passed it on to my daughter. I don't want her to worry about her weight and yet I DO."

She began to cry. And then the mother next to her also started to cry as she realized she'd done the same thing to her daughter.

At each focus group, we asked moms: "Is there a part of your daughter's body or face that she does not like?" Fifty percent said yes. Then we asked them, "How do *you* feel about that part of your body or face?" Twenty-eight percent said they also did not like it. Seventeen percent were uncertain.

These mothers may be passing on lies about beauty.

One study revealed that 80 percent of ten-year-old girls had already been on diets to lose weight. Anorexia and bulimia are on the rise. This research was referenced in a *Wall Street Journal* article linking the ways mothers think about their bodies to the aftermath of adult

> **TRUTH #5** The beauty that matters most to God is on the inside of me.

Do you love the way you look? If your immediate answer is no, you're not alone. The lie I'm about to reveal is kind of related to the last one. A lot of girls say, **"I'm not pretty enough!"** But the beauty problem is so big, it deserves its very own Truth statement.

Almost half of the girls we talked to are not happy with how they look.[1] When we asked them what part of their face or body they didn't like, the number one answer was their weight. Sometimes they thought they weighed too much, and sometimes too little.

THEY WROTE THINGS LIKE:

🍎 **"I think I'm fat and ugly."**

🍎 **"I like my freckles, but I wish I were taller and weighed more."**

I know this is partly because we are surrounded by pretty girls on TV, on YouTube, in movies, and in ads. And, because these girls get a lot of attention and sometimes become famous, it's easy to compare ourselves to them.

It's also easy to believe a big lie.

▶ **LIE: "PRETTY GIRLS ARE WORTH MORE."** ◀

Let's ask an important question to fight this lie: **Are these "pretty girls" really as perfect as they look?** The Bible warns that beauty can **sometimes** fool you and that it **always** fades. There are often so many special effects applied to photos of "pretty" girls that if you met them in real life you might not recognize them. This is what one of them said about a photo that was supposed to show her with no makeup.

Sadie Robertson, Louisiana, United States

" . . . the director of the shoot took a quick look at me and said, 'Nope this girl does not have the face to pull off . . . no makeup!' They proceeded to spend around two hours making it look as though I had no makeup on. Let's be real I did NOT wake up like that."[2]

It took two hours to put on Sadie's makeup for her "no make-up" photo!

The Bible tells us things like hairstyles, nice clothes, and jewelry are not what God considers beautiful. The physical qualities that are so important to us are not worth much to God.

Let's find Truth in the Bible to replace that lie. ▼

TRUTH NUGGET:

"The LORD doesn't see things the way you see them. People judge by outward appearance, but the LORD looks at the heart." (1 Samuel 16:7)

I so want you to concentrate on the beauty that matters most: your heart. You become most beautiful to God when you get excited about wearing things like kindness, helpfulness, and cheerfulness, rather than some cool new shoes, or a great lip gloss.

Nowhere does the Bible say it's bad to want to be beautiful or to appreciate beauty in someone else. But it is wrong to go crazy over physical beauty without being concerned with the beauty of our hearts. So spend time learning how to be helpful. Ask someone to help you be more truthful. Or practice giving by saving some money and giving it to your church or to someone who has a special need. These are the things God finds beautiful!

daughters' beliefs about theirs. Thirty to forty percent of women think about body image every day and almost half of them say it is because their mothers did. They resent their mothers for it.[3]

I have to wonder how many of those same women are equally concerned about their inner beauty. Are they mindful of being submissive, helpful, kind, forgiving, and cheerful? If, as mothers, we are not focused on the kind of beauty that never fades, how can we expect our daughters to be?

Conversation Tip for Truth #5:

We are quick to tell our daughters they are physically beautiful, but often fail to affirm their internal qualities. Tell your daughter about the inner beauty you see in her. Maybe she is helpful in the kitchen or loves to read to her little brother or is diligent with her homework. Point out a quality of inner beauty, and make a note to affirm it regularly.

NOTES FOR MOM

About Truth #6:

As your daughter enters into the phase of life where she individuates and becomes her own self, she may develop some willpower. This is good, because it gives her strength upon which to plant her growing biblical convictions. It also helps her to see needs and responsibly meet them without needing direction. For example, she might rise from the dinner table and start unloading a full dishwasher so she can help you clean the table, or she might make her bed without being nagged. (Sounds nice, right?) These are behaviors of a maturing tween girl.

But many girls don't want to use their maturity to be responsible; instead, they want to use it to have stuff. The willpower shows up here too!

How can you know the difference between healthy willpower and sinful entitlement?

Here's the litmus test: When you refuse your daughter something—going to a sleepover or buying some new jeans—it should cause some natural sadness and disappointment, without manifesting in the silent treatment, a tantrum, or full-out fury. The latter are immature, self-centered, sinful responses to authority.

TRUTH #6 You're ready for more responsibility.

Did you know that "teenagers" and "tweens" are actually modern inventions? A long time ago those words didn't exist. You know what did? Responsibility!

Way back when Jesus was alive, a 12-year-old **wanted** to earn responsibility. He or she was expected to be wise, mature, and responsible.

A girl might walk a long distance to fetch water for her family each morning, or make bread for the family dinner each evening. She knew that not doing those things would result in a thirsty or hungry family. Back then, girls who were 8 or 9 were thinking about learning to **DO** things.

It took nearly 2,000 years for that to change. Kids became less interested in responsibility when they were distracted by new things like cars,

RESPONSIBILITY

"doing things that you are expected to do and accepting the results of your actions"[4]

movie theaters, and makeup. As people started to make these things, they also invented the words "teen" and "tween"[5] so they could convince those age groups that they needed to buy stuff. They told girls that they needed **things**. The result? Today, a lot of girls want to **HAVE** things.

And sometimes they are things adults—parents, teachers, or lawmakers—think girls are not ready to have yet. **Some** girls think their world has too many rules if they can't have the freedom to have anything they want.

And when they think about that
a whole lot, they begin to believe a lie.

▶ LIE: "I NEED MORE FREEDOM." ◀

37% OF GIRLS SAY THEY NEED MORE FREEDOM.

If you are one of them, I have a question to ask: What do you want to do with your freedom? Circle one.

I want freedom to HAVE things like makeup or a phone and to go to parties.

OR

I want freedom so I can DO things for others and be trusted with more responsibilities.

I hope you circled the second one, but I'm thankful for your honesty if you circled the first one. Based on my conversations with tween girls, a lot of them would most likely circle the first one because they grumbled really loud when they said things like:

"I HAVE to do chores!"

"My parents make me do a ridiculous amount of jobs, but they don't let me have anything good like a cellphone or makeup!"

It sounded to me like some of them were complaining about having responsibilities. Time to put grumbling attitudes into the Truth Lab. ▼

TRUTH NUGGET:
"Do everything without complaining and arguing."
(Philippians 2:14)

Nancy

The time will come when you are in charge of decisions, but you must prove your readiness. Look for chances to practice responsibility, not freedom.

NOTES FOR MOM

While these behaviors may be "normal" in our culture, they are not okay and are evidence that she wants things and privileges, rather than responsibility and trust.

Conversation Tip for Truth #6:

Responsibility isn't necessarily fun, but it does yield an internal sense of accomplishment. Tell your daughter about responsibilities that are difficult for you. (For me, it would be grocery shopping and folding the laundry. These are both so repetitive that they feel like a waste of time. I used to dread them.)

Next, tell her how you have chosen to approach that duty with a good heart, free of complaining and arguing. (I use grocery time and laundry time to pray for my family. As I select their favorite food at the store or fold a piece of their clothing, I talk to God about them. This has changed my heart big time!)

Spend some time listening to your daughter's heart about what responsibilities are difficult for her. Help her develop some creative ways to approach them.

NOTES FOR MOM

Since the assignments for your daughter's lab work are the same regardless of the chapter content, I only provided ideas about how to interact with your daughter at the end of chapter 4. You can refer back to those "Notes for Mom" on pages 72–73 if you need a refresher.

Instead of complaining, "I **HAVE** to do chores," a mature girl says, "I **GET** to do chores." It is a good thing to be helpful to those you love and live with. Being a tween means that it's time for you to begin to grow up. Even Jesus had to **GROW** in wisdom and maturity (Luke 2:52). He didn't just have His freedom given to Him because He was the Son of God!

PUT ON YOUR LAB COAT

Grab your pencils. It's your turn to work in our Truth Lab.

THE LIE

I'm not good enough.

Beautiful girls are worth more.

I need more freedom.

THE TRUTH

• God chose you. (Ephesians 1:7)

• We are not "good enough" without God, but He is our "enough." (2 Corinthians 3:5)

• You are wonderfully made. (Psalm 139:13–14; Ephesians 2:10)

• God looks at my heart. (1 Samuel 16:7)

• You're ready for more responsibility. (Luke 2:52)

• God wants you to embrace responsibility without grumbling or complaining. (Philippians 2:14)

TRUTH LAB REVIEW

NOTES FOR MOM

*Got a thought?
Don't lose it.
Write it here*

TELLING MYSELF THE TRUTH
It's your turn to be the author!

🖤 Have you believed any lies about yourself? Put an X on top of any of **THE LIES** in this chapter that you have believed.

🖤 What Truth do you need to think about **all the time**, EVERY DAY? Look at **THE TRUTH** we dug up together, and circle what seems important to dwell on.

🖤 Next, begin to think about it **all the time**, EVERY DAY. You can start by writing a prayer to God, a helpful Bible verse, or some ideas you don't want to forget in the space below.

Helping Zoey Believe Truth
It's time to give Zoey some advice!

Zoey got picked last and felt really bad about it. In fact, she started to believe some lies, because she said she "deserved" it. If you could encourage her, how would you help her believe Truth?

Truth and Lies about My Family

Pray like this:

Our Father in heaven,
may your name be kept holy.
May your Kingdom come soon.
May your will be done on earth,
as it is in heaven.
Give us today the food we need,
and forgive us our sins,
as we have forgiven those who sin against us.
And don't let us yield to temptation,
but rescue us from the evil one.

(Matthew 6:9–13)

What we often call "The Lord's Prayer" was actually intended to be "our prayer"— given to us by the Lord Himself, to teach us how we should pray. We can use this model to intercede for our families.

It takes no persuasion for me to recite the parts of the prayer that benefit my family and me.

When Bob and I were a young married couple, with one baby and an empty cupboard, I remember asking the Lord literally for daily bread. I asked all day long. What a joy it was to come home and find a check from an anonymous friend who had heard that we'd done some free marketing for a Christian high school.

I also remember asking Him to forgive me for the sexual past that I brought to my pure, holy marriage bed. With a heavy heart, I begged God to fix my marriage—and me—for a decade. It's been a glorious unfolding to experience God's grace and healing in my life, and then to have Him use me to help other women experience restoration.

With tears burning my eyes at times, I have prayed for my young adult children as I asked God not to let them be led into temptation. There are so many lures and traps out there.

These things are easy for us to pray. We naturally plead with God to give, provide, and protect.

However, it's not so easy to speak the parts of this prayer that require our surrender and obedience. Things like: "May your kingdom come. May your will be done on earth."

The word come is an imperative verb. That is to say it is a call to action. While God's kingdom had already been established on earth (Psalm 103), there was and is a sense in which it has not yet come. Pastor John Piper says the prayer is one petitioning God to "continue transforming the world into a place where everyone obeys him perfectly and joyfully."[1] In other words, we're not only supposed to be asking for this earth to look a little like heaven, but we must be cooperating with Him to make it happen. Best-selling author Philip Yancey said we could just as easily pray it this way:

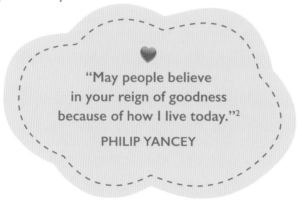

"May people believe in your reign of goodness because of how I live today."[2]

PHILIP YANCEY

It's hard to live well in this world. And no one sees me not living well more frequently than my family. I've hurt them with my words, my sins, my selfishness, and my ambition. Can you identify? Of course, you can. I was not surprised when I read some of the comments girls wrote when they were asked about their families.

- *My brother hurts me, and my parents yell at me.*

- *My dad lives far, far away and doesn't see me.*

- *We fight more than I like.*

- *My dad is in prison so we live with my mom only.*

These are broken lives. Just as my life is broken in places. And just as yours is, I imagine. And yet! Even though God knew we would be broken, He chose for marriage and family to be a picture of His love. Several times in Scripture it is written that a man and his wife would become "one flesh," so that they could display the love of Christ for His bride, the church (Genesis 2:24; Mark 10:8; Ephesians 5:31–32). This is true even though many of us have experienced pain in our marriages (or in the lack of a marriage). It's true even if your parents' marriage . . . or yours . . . has been painful or ended badly. In spite of our brokenness, marriage is a relationship that God created to showcase His love for us.

In addition, we are called His children (John 1:12). He reveals Himself as our *Father*. The word *adoption* describes the act of salvation as we are grafted into the family of God (Ephesians 1:5). A family functioning the way God intended, helps a lost world see God and His kingdom.

No wonder Satan attacks our families so persistently.

I want to suggest that the most effective way you can bid God's kingdom come to earth may not be through serving as your church's children's ministry director . . . or singing on a praise team . . . or spending your life on a foreign mission field . . . or writing that book that's burning inside of you. No. These things, of course, do matter, but there is no more powerful way you can bid His kingdom come than by giving a lost world pause to believe in His reign of goodness because of the goodness they see in your family.

You don't have to have a perfect family. You simply have to keep bringing your family back to Jesus and His Truth when the broken pieces need fixing.

TALKING WITH GOD:

Use Matthew 6:9-13 to bring your family before the Lord. Ask Him to provide your daily material needs, pardon your sins, and protect you from the evil one. Then, ask God to bring His kingdom to this earth by displaying His goodness in your family. Write out specific thoughts in the lines provided.

Pray like this:

Our Father in heaven,
  may your name be kept holy.
May your Kingdom come soon.
May your will be done on earth,
  as it is in heaven.
Give us today the food we need,
and forgive us our sins,
  as we have forgiven those who sin against us.
And don't let us yield to temptation,
  but rescue us from the evil one.

(Matthew 6:9–13)

_____

_____

_____

_____

_____

TALKING WITH YOUR GIRL:

Now that you've prayed, invite your daughter to read chapter 6 in her book while you review the same content here in your book. I've written a few notes for you in the margins. You might want to add your own notes to help prompt you when it's time to discuss this chapter with your girl.

Lies about Family

CHAPTER 6

Does your family put the "funk" in dysfunction? Make a few notes. You may need them!

> Argh! My little brother and I got into a fight. **AGAIN!** We're always arguing. My friend told me **EVERYONE** in the world fights with their little brothers and it's no big deal. If that's true, why do I feel so bad about it? **This is the same friend that told me to lie to my parents about downloading that app!!! I don't think it's really okay to fight with my brother.**

Just like Zoey, maybe you fight with your siblings, or maybe even your parents. Sometimes a family can feel like a gift you wish you could take back. But there's no return department that accepts parents or siblings! So, we have to sort through the lies about our families. Here's an important Truth to believe about your family.

NOTES FOR MOM

About Truth #7:

Thirty-seven percent of the girls we surveyed thought their family had too many rules. They wanted to be like everyone else—to do sleepovers, have smart-phones, and listen to whatever music they pleased. They wanted to be "normal."

Normal is overrated! That's something I hope to plant into your daughter's head—and yours. So often we measure our family and our children's behavior by the families around us and the behavior of other children we know. That's not a good idea.

Giving into cultural trends may be normal, but it's seldom God's best. You have established rules for your daughter's protection, and should continue to lovingly enforce them.

Sibling rivalry is another area where the idea of "normal" came up with the girls who took my survey. Sinful, selfish conflict may be normal, but it's not God's best.

Let's use God's Truth to plant an understanding that different is good.

TRUTH #7 Your family is different, and that is good.

Think back to the last lie, **"I need more freedom."** One of the reasons girls feel the need for freedom is because of the rules in their family. Sometimes these rules are different from the rules their friends' families have.

This makes some girls believe a lie.

▶ **LIE: "MY FAMILY IS SOOOO WEIRD."** ◀

But rules were not the **only** reason they believed this lie. I counted **171 reasons** why girls believed they had a super crazy family.

HERE ARE JUST A FEW OF THE THINGS GIRLS SAID:

🍎 "We do not eat sugar."

🍎 "It's a foster family and we have a lot of kids."

🍎 "I'm adopted."

🍎 "We are different colors."

🍎 "We're a pastor's family, and it's abnormal."

🍎 "We live in India."

🍎 "We raise GOATS! GOATS!"

🍎 "We are HUGE! There are seven people in this HOUSE!!!"

🍎 "We live on a farm and we are homeschooled."

🍎 "My parents are artists, so we are all a bit weird."

🍎 "I'm so different. My family is so indescribable."

A lot of these girls said their lives would be better if their families were "**just** a little" more like everyone else's. They **want** to be normal, but is that what's best? For example, many of them reported fighting with their siblings . . . a lot!

🍎 **81% of girls fight with their siblings.**

When we asked how they felt about it, there were two opinions that were most common.

🍎 **47% said, "I wish we didn't."**

🍎 **34% said, "It's okay. It's normal!"**

Some girls may think it's normal to fight with your siblings, BUT that doesn't mean it's okay. The Bible instructs us to "do all" we can "to live in peace with everyone." That includes our brothers and sisters. When we fight without doing all we can to avoid it just because it's "normal," we are not living the way God created us to live. Being normal is not **best**.

NOTES FOR MOM

Conversation Tip for Truth #7:

Remember, the word *why* becomes important to tweens as they are developing their belief system. Take time to tell your daughter how you came to a significant decision for your family, such as *why* you live in an unusual place, have a tight budget, or embrace foster children. It may help her understand your heart, and hopefully enter into your mission.

For example, it *is* difficult to be the sole biological child in a home with multiple foster children. Understanding *why* you obeyed the calling may be what makes carrying the burden easier.

NORMAL IS OVERRATED.

But you may still say, "But I can't eat sugar! What's the sin in **that**?" Or "My family has GOATS! Does it have to be that way?" Or "My family is too big. Why does my mom keep having babies?" Those things can make you feel weird, too. So, we still haven't solved your problem, have we?

Oh, look! I see we have dug ourselves straight down to a truth nugget. And just in time.

TRUTH NUGGET: "Don't copy the behavior and customs of this world, but let God transform you into a new person by changing the way you think. Then you will learn to know God's will for you, which is good and pleasing and perfect." (Romans 12:2)

The Bible tells us we are NOT supposed to be like everyone else. Instead, we should let God be in charge of how we think. The difference that should be seen in a Christian family is summed up well by a girl who wrote:

"We don't do what people who are not Christians do."

🌼 AMEN!

You might say, "But what does this have to do with not eating sugar?" Or maybe you want to know: "How does this Truth help me if I have the **HUGEST** family in church, and feel like we're kind of a freak show?"

Well, there are **SOME** things your parents do because God leads them to decisions that are unique. And when you really think about it, some of the things that make your life a little different are super cool. God asks some parents to adopt and some to be foster parents. He asks some to be missionaries in India and others to lead a church in Ohio.

And there are also **SOME** things your parents do just because they like it or believe it is best for your family, and it helps them practice being different. They might eat differently or be artistic or raise goats.

Your family is different. That's a good thing!

Of course, sometimes the differences in your family are truly painful. Let's talk about that next.

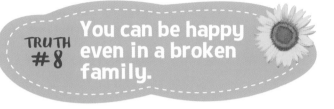

TRUTH #8 You can be happy even in a broken family.

Some girls thought their family was weird because of divorce, overworking, sickness, and even death. In extreme cases, girls even questioned whether or not their parents loved them. A lot of our families are very broken.

▶ "My dad is in the hospital a lot. My mom is always angry, but I have my dog so that helps."

▶ "Dad is in jail."

▶ "I have a sick sister, so we're late for almost everything."

▶ "My dad is never home because he works third shift, and when he is home he just sleeps and gets angry."

▶ "My dad left us."

▶ "My parents are divorced."

I understand your pain. I have had some sad things happen in my own family that caused a lot of tears. It's okay to be sad when your family feels broken. God sees your pain. The Bible says He "keeps track of all [our] sorrows," and He has "recorded each one in [His] book" (Psalm 56:8). He would only do that if He cared and wanted to help you.

NOTES FOR MOM

Conversation Tip for Truth #8:

Perhaps your daughter doesn't have a challenging family situation, but she struggles with contentment. Today it is rare to find someone who is truly content. It seems the more prosperous a culture, the less content and the more unhappy people are likely to be.

We have so much to be grateful for. According to global statistics, anyone with a roof over his or her head and a meal on his or her table daily is richer than 93 percent of the world.[3] If you had the money to buy this book and the education to read it, you're pretty wealthy!

Ask your daughter if there is something she wishes she could have or be. Then, ask her if she is willing to be content if she never gets what she's hoping for.

If she says no, accept her honest answer. Use that to evaluate how you are parenting.

Are you modeling contentment?

Do you let her have everything she wants, without opportunities to learn contentment?

What can you do differently to help her learn this Truth?

At the same time, He doesn't want us to **give in** to being constantly sad. It can be tempting to dwell on the sadness. That is, to think about it **all the time**, **EVERY DAY**, and maybe even believe it will never change.

Here's the problem with that: you might begin to believe a lie.

▶ LIE: "MY FAMILY IS TOO BROKEN FOR ME TO EVER BE HAPPY." ◀

When you believe the lie that you cannot be happy unless everything in your family and life are okay, you put your trust in the wrong places. Jesus wants you to hope in **HIM**, not in your family. The Truth is that happiness is not found in family, or in any human relationship. True joy can only be found in Jesus.

Let's dig deep to discover God's Truth. ▼

 TRUTH NUGGET: "I have learned how to be content with whatever I have." (Philippians 4:11)

Let me explain the word **content**. It's a little different from the kind of happiness you feel on Christmas morning. It's not the kind of happy you feel when all your friends come to your birthday party. It's a different kind of happy. It's quiet and peaceful. It's kind of like feeling okay.

The man who wrote the book of Philippians in the Bible understood that we may not be able to control the things that happen to us, but the things that happen don't have to control us. He went through some hard things, like being put in jail for talking about Jesus. Even there, he was content.

CONTENTMENT
"a state of peaceful happiness"[4]

The Truth is that if you are not content with your family now, you may not be content your whole life because our world is broken, and bad things do happen.*

Nine-year-old Talia knows what it feels like to have a broken family. She was born to a mom who didn't have much money. They shared a bed, and Talia kept all her clothes in a garbage bag.

---

* There are some important exceptions to being content. If someone is hurting you, touching you in ways that make you feel uncomfortable, or saying a lot of cruel things to you, TELL SOMEONE! That is called abuse, and you should never be content with it.

NOTES FOR MOM

Pray with your daughter, asking God to help you both to be grateful for what you do have and patient concerning what you don't.

Talia Saum, Minnesota, United States

"I would often wake up, there was barely anything to eat. Sometimes my mom wasn't even at home, and I would just go back to sleep until she came home."

Things went from bad to worse when Talia had to go live in a home for children because her mom could not take care of her. Soon she went to live with a foster family. There, she heard about Jesus.

"I love that Jesus loves everyone no matter what they have done. He changed my life so much."

Talia was adopted by her foster family when she was 7 years old, but there is always a part of her that is aware of how broken families can be.

"I pray for my birth parents to become Christians every night. And because of all I have been through, I like to do things for others now. I don't just want to think of myself, and what I need. I know what it's like to be hurt, and I know who I can trust—God."

Talia has learned what it means to be content. Her story inspires me so much.

Nancy

We may not be able to control the things that happen to us, but the things that happen to us don't have to control us.

About Truth #9:

Let's review something I wrote about way back in chapter 3.

I asked moms in my focus groups this question: *Does your daughter display a belief in submission by the way she obeys you and other authorities in her life?*

Seven percent said *yes*, she always obeys.

Sixteen percent said *no*, she rarely obeys.

Seventy-six percent said *sometimes*—she tries but struggles.

Some moms recognized that even when their daughters did obey, their motivation was fear of consequences rather than a deep sense of right and wrong.

If your girl is going to grow into a friend who compassionately cares for others, a wife who respects her husband, and an employee who responds effectively to her boss, her motivation to obey needs to grow out of a deep root of Truth. This is a topic where you need to intentionally slow down, hear her heart, and help her to gain understanding about why *obeying*, *honoring*, and *submitting* are good words.

TRUTH #9 **God gives you joy when you honor your parents.**

My mom was one of my best friends when I was growing up. A relationship like that is something to cherish, because not every girl shares a special friendship with her mom. If you're a girl who wishes she had this, you should know that even those of us who are friends with our moms have experienced the pain of feeling misunderstood.

For example, you might have a perfect day where you laugh a lot and eat cookie dough 'til you can't move. Just when you feel like your mom is the coolest thing on the planet, **things go bad!** You ask your best-friend-of-a-mom to go to a movie that "everyone else is seeing." But she says no. And then, she says, "I'm not raising one of the bunch. I'm raising a top banana!"

That's a real thing my mom said to me over and over again when I wanted to do something "everyone else was

doing." I admit that I often dramatically stomped off. Sometimes I gave my mom the silent treatment. **That wasn't cool! Why did I act that way?**

Well, sometimes I believed this lie.

▶ LIE: "MY PARENTS JUST DON'T GET ME." ◀

I sometimes felt like my parents were so old that they just couldn't understand me! Have you ever felt that way? This lie might show up with some other lies, such as: "I don't have to honor my parents because they're so old-fashioned," or "My mom (or dad) doesn't love me," or "My mom is **supposed** to be my best friend!" No matter what form it takes, you are at risk of believing this lie when you don't like the way your parents are . . . well, **parenting**.

What comes next is often ugly. (Did I mention stomping off, the silent treatment, arguing, throwing a fit, and being plain **RUDE** to my awesome mom?) We humans don't naturally obey, respect, and honor, do we? (Things just got real!)

I have a truth nugget for you. It's not very fancy because we just need straight-up truth. ▼

TRUTH NUGGET:

"Children, obey your parents because you belong to the Lord, for this is the right thing to do. 'Honor your father and mother.' This is the first commandment with a promise: If you honor your father and mother, 'things will go well for you, and you will have a long life on earth.'" (Ephesians 6:1–3)

This verse doesn't need a lot of explaining. You are supposed to honor your parents, which means to treat them with respect.

▼ LET ME SHARE FIVE PRACTICAL WAYS YOU CAN DO THIS

NOTES FOR MOM

More than one mom confessed that her daughter's disrespect was a result of the poor example she'd set for her. If that's you, put this book down and pick up *Lies Women Believe*. Go to chapter 7 where Nancy did a stellar job in bringing my heart to a place of conviction when it comes to submitting to my husband and his needs. Though the chapter deals with marriage, the concept of submission is for all of us no matter our marital state.

Big Question:

Do you believe the words *obey*, *honor*, and *submit* are good?

NOTES FOR MOM

Conversation Tip for Truth #9:

I know you already know the answer, but ask your daughter if submission and obedience are difficult for her. Try to help her figure out *why* they are so hard. (Remember, there is often a lie deep down under the sinful behavior.) Does she feel like she is losing control? Is she afraid you don't understand her? Are there issues of jealousy between her and another sibling? Dig deep to figure out what Truth she specifically needs.

Discuss the list in her book of ways to practice submission.

5

PRACTICAL WAYS TO HONOR YOUR PARENTS

Accept their decisions, even if you don't love the decisions they make.
(Don't stomp off, argue, or give them the silent treatment.)

Ask for their advice because they are wise.
(I know you naturally want to ask your BFF about boys, friends, or God. But your mom and dad know a lot more on those topics.)

Speak well of them in front of others.
(You don't get to stop honoring them when they aren't around.)

Be respectful when you disagree.
(It's okay to tell your mom or dad that you don't like a decision they make, or that your opinion is different. Just do it nicely, and obey their decision even if you can't win them over.)

Forgive them when they sometimes get it wrong.
(They're imperfect and sinful, just like you. So be quick to forgive them. They've probably forgiven you a time or two!)

Here's the really great thing that happens when you start to practice this hard task of honoring your father and mother: **it feels good!**

It's called joy. It's the good feeling you get inside when things outside don't go your way. It comes from doing the right thing. This makes sense because our Truth Nugget tells us "things will go well for you" when you honor your parents.

Let me tell you an important fact:

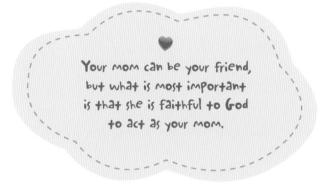

Your mom can be your friend, but what is most important is that she is faithful to God to act as your mom.

Above all, she is your parent. Let's not forget your dad. I know lots of girls with special father/daughter relationships. That should be treasured, but you should still remain faithful to honoring, respecting, and treating them both like parents.

Got a thought?
Don't lose it.
Write it here.

NOTES FOR MOM

Since the assignments for your daughter's lab work are the same regardless of the chapter content, I only provided ideas about how to interact with your daughter at the end of chapter 4. You can refer back to those "Notes for Mom" on pages 72–73 if you need a refresher.

PUT ON YOUR LAB COAT

Grab your pencils.
It's your turn to work in our Truth Lab.

THE LIE

My family is weird.

My family is too broken to be happy.

My parents just don't get me.

THE TRUTH

• **Your family is different. That is good.** (Romans 12:2)

• **Normal is overrated.** (Ephesians 4:17,19–20)

• **You should stick out.** (Philippians 2:15)

• **You can be happy even in a broken family.** (Philippians 4:12–13)

• **God wants you to trust in Him, not your family.** (Psalm 118:8)

• **You can learn to be content no matter what.** (Philippians 4:11,13)

• **Both your parents are to be honored.** (Ephesians 6:1–2)

• **Obey your parents.** (Ephesians 6:1–2)

• **God gives you joy when you honor your parents.** (Ephesians 6:3)

THINKING ABOUT TRUTH

TELLING MYSELF THE TRUTH
It's your turn to be the author!

💜 Have you believed any of these lies about your family? Put an X on top of any of **THE LIES** in this chapter that you have believed.

💜 What Truth do you need to think about **all the time**, EVERY DAY? Look at **THE TRUTH** we dug up together. Now circle what seems important for you personally to dwell on.

💜 Next, begin to think about it **all the time**, EVERY DAY. You can start by writing a prayer to God, a helpful Bible verse, or some ideas you don't want to forget in the space below.

Helping Zoey Believe Truth
It's time to give Zoey some advice!

Zoey's friend told her that it's normal to fight with siblings.
Do you agree or disagree? Why or why not?
What do you think Zoey should do about fighting with her brother?

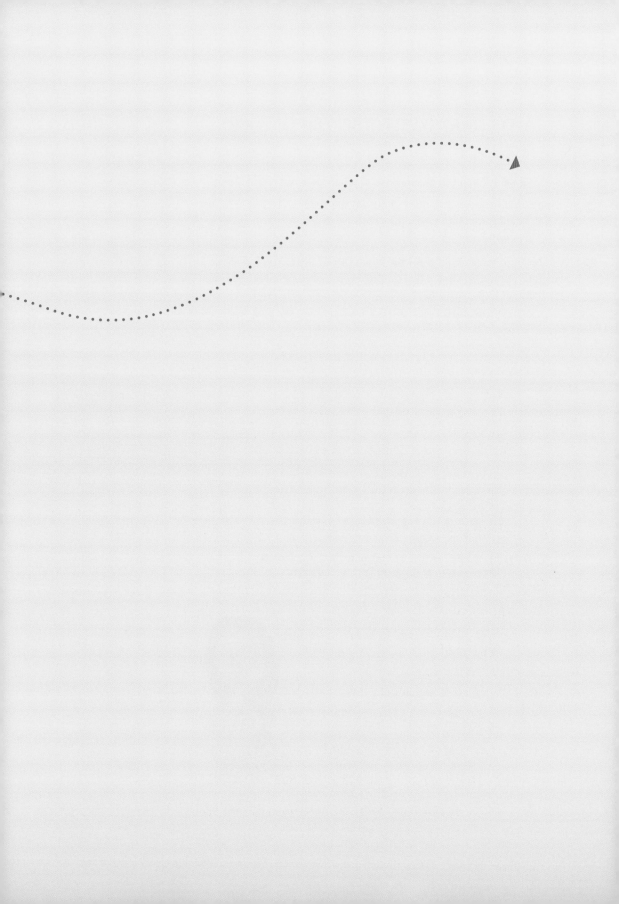

Truth and Lies about Sin

When my Lexi was seven or eight years old, she handed me a worn-out stuffed beanbag cat. With tear-filled eyes, she confessed that she'd stolen it from our previous church in Missouri.

I quickly did some mental math. We had moved to Pennsylvania nearly three years earlier. This meant my sweet girl had been carrying around more than a stolen toy. She'd also been burdened by the weight of a heavy secret for a long time.

I prayed, *Lord, how do I apply grace to this situation?*

Then, I listened to my daughter's heart. It was as complicated and messy as things can be for a little one who's been beaten up by the enemy's favorite tool: shame.

Lexi felt compelled to write a letter to Pastor Tim Cook, apologizing and asking for his forgiveness. So, she did. Next, we headed to the store and bought an identical beanbag cat. We packaged it up and shipped it, along with the worn-out one and my daughter's handwritten confession.

A few weeks later, a letter arrived in our mailbox from that dear man. Pastor Cook's grace-filled note extended forgiveness to Lexi. He also shared how proud he was of her for confessing. He encouraged my girl never to be afraid to tell someone when she sins.

Most of us *are* afraid to tell another person about our sin at some point in our lives.

Fifty-four percent of the seven to twelve-year-old girls who took our survey were hiding a secret about sin.

Some of the girls wrote comments defining their sin. In specific instances, it was stuff I'm fairly confident their parents already knew about, such as:

- *I blame things on my brother that I actually did.*

- *I have a habit of talking back to my parents.*

- *I read at night. I'm not supposed to, but I try to hide the book. Most of the time I succeed.*

But not all of the secrets girls hid were so innocuous. Many of them wrote comments revealing deep battles with shame, fear, and temptation. Like these:

🍎 *I feel like I hate my mom and I can't wait to grow up. I'm mean at school to someone who has been mean to me.*

🍎 *There's this girl who calls herself a Christian, but she doesn't act like one. She's always talking about sex. She looks at porn. She shows me inappropriate videos. I'm around her a lot because she goes to my homeschool co-op. I sin by letting her say and do those things and not telling her they're wrong. I'm scared she'll hate me, and she's the only person who talks to me.*

Sometimes the secrets they carried were about someone else's sin and temptation.

🍎 *Right now I'm really worried because my friend that is 11 is talking about a list that her friend has of boys she wants to smash. That means have sex with. But I really think she is talking about herself.*

Due to the confidential nature of how we surveyed girls, I could not reach out to these tweens or their parents. (Oh, how I wanted to!) But I can sound an alarm and encourage you to have conversations with your daughter to make your home a safe place for her to talk to you about sin.

You see, I think kids don't talk about sin because *we* don't talk about it. At least not our own. To make matters worse, it's likely that your daughter has overheard someone gossiping about another person's sin.

Christian psychologist Mark R. McMinn believes that we don't genuinely want to discuss and understand sin. He writes this about the dilemma:

💜

"This is not just a mainstream psychology problem; it has affected Christian psychology as well. Philip Monroe, a faculty member at Biblical Theological Seminary, recently noted that only 43 of the 1,143 articles published in *Journal of Psychology and Theology* and *Journal of Psychology and Christianity* have been related to sin, and only four of those are related to the effects or treatment of sinful patterns. I wonder if we lost the language of sin because the language of psychology took its place."

MARK R. McMINN, PhD[1]

Here's where I need to refer back to a psychological term we've already explored: *self-esteem*. Self-esteem has its origins in the late 1800s when a psychologist coined it. However, it gained steam in the 1940s when Abraham Maslow included self-esteem and self-actualization at the pinnacle of his hierarchy of human needs. Since then, it's been credited by the psychological community as a common denominator in individuals achieving success.

Here's the thing: the language of self-esteem is based on how we feel about ourselves. I'm trying to help your daughter know that her feelings aren't supposed to be governing her behavior because they aren't often accurate or truthful. What is true is God's Word, and in the seventh century BC, God inspired Joshua to write down His recipe for success: ▼

 TRUTH NUGGET: "Study this Book of Instruction continually. Meditate on it day and night so you will be sure to obey everything written in it. Only then will you prosper and succeed in all you do." (Joshua 1:8)

"This Book of Instruction" contains God's guidelines for living. His rules. And then it makes an audacious declaration: obedience—not self-esteem or actualization—is God's recipe for success and prosperity.

It's time to reclaim the language of the Bible. Here's a definition that your daughter learned in chapter 2 of *Lies Girls Believe*:

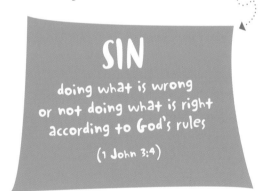

SIN

doing what is wrong
or not doing what is right
according to God's rules

(1 John 3:4)

Sin is doing things our way instead of God's way. It's allowing our emotions and desires to decide what we will and will not do, rather than trusting God's good plan. In a way, it's focusing too much on ourselves.

While talking about God's rules is an integral part of the language of sin, an equally important concept is God's grace.

If you recall, in chapter 1, I asked you to choose between two parenting styles. I wrote this:

Will you be a mother who merely restrains your daughter's external behavior so it appears to conform to Truth?

OR

Will you nurture her in Truth so that her external behavior is an outgrowth of what is planted deeply inside of her heart?

I encouraged you to select the second option, and warned that parenting this way requires liberal doses of grace. Well, here's your chance to put that into action. As you work through this chapter, your daughter might confess a sin to you. Slowly, tenderly, lovingly hear her confession, be grateful for it, and nurture her in Truth! That is to say, apply a liberal dose of grace.

TALKING WITH GOD:

Use Joshua 1:8 to write a prayer to God for your daughter's success. Ask Him to give her a desire to know God's rules through the study of His Word and to give her a heart that longs to be obedient. Write out your prayer in the lines below.

Study this Book of Instruction continually. Meditate on it
day and night so you will be sure to obey everything written in it.
Only then will you prosper and succeed in all you do.
(Joshua 1:8)

_____

_____

_____

_____

_____

TALKING WITH YOUR GIRL:

Now that you've prayed, invite your daughter to read chapter 7 in her book while you review the same content here in your book. I've written a few notes for you in the margins. You might want to add your own notes to help prompt you when it's time to discuss this chapter with your girl.

Lies about Sin

CHAPTER 7

NOTES FOR MOM

Remember, this space is for your notes.

Gigi's my best friend. We tell each other **EVERYTHING**! Sometimes we just hang out for hours. But . . . not anymore. She **LIED** to me! Gigi said she was the **only** one invited to Emma's for a sleepover, but it turns out everyone in my class except ME was invited. When I called Gigi on it, she acted like it was **NO BIG DEAL**! She told me she lied so my feelings wouldn't be hurt!!!! She actually said that sometimes it's good to lie. I'm so mad! I feel like having a sleepover and not inviting her!

Zoey has discovered something important. Gigi's lie made her feel lonely. That's the thing about lies, they make us feel far away from others, including God. (And, by the way, even when we are trying to protect someone's feelings, lying is always a sin.) Let's dig into Truth #10!

TRUTH #10 Sin separates you from God.

I **know what it's like to feel the separation that sin creates.** When I was young, we weren't allowed to eat or drink in my dad's office. One super hot summer day, I needed to work in there, and I decided to take my drink with me. **BIG MISTAKE!** I spilled red juice all over the carpet. I cleaned and prayed, hoping my dad wouldn't notice.

But he did!

He asked me what happened. I just shrugged my shoulders as if to say, "I don't know."

It worked!!! My dad didn't punish me, or anything. I thought the whole thing was no big deal. **I had heard of worse sins than disobeying my dad or lying.**

Some girls, like me, think **their** sin is no big deal when people around them do things that seem worse. It's almost like we try to grade sin. Things like stealing or murder seem like **BIGGER, BADDER SINS**. Things like that get a big, ugly F. But does that mean things like lying or cheating or grumbling or being mean only get a B-?

Maybe you have believed the lie that I did.

▶ **LIE: "MY SIN ISN'T THAT BIG OF A DEAL."** ◀

If you have, you are not alone.

23% of girls believe that the sins of others were bigger and badder than their own.

THESE GIRLS SAID THINGS LIKE:

- 🍎 I lie about cleaning my whole room or about brushing my teeth. It's really dumb.
- 🍎 I blame stuff on my brother that I actually did.
- 🍎 I have a habit of talking back to my parents.

If only we could understand that every single sin is a big deal. Every time we sin, we choose our way instead of God's way.

Do you remember how Adam and Eve hid from God after they sinned? It's because they began to feel far away from Him.

After I sinned by lying to my dad, I started to feel far away from him **and** from God too. The fun friendship I shared when my dad and I trained our German Shepherd dogs was awkward, and even going to dog shows together felt lonely. And when it came to God, I could hardly pray.

No matter how small or big a sin may seem, the result is the same.

 TRUTH NUGGET: "But your sins have separated you from your God." (Isaiah 59:2a NIrV)

Are there any sins in your life that you don't think are a big deal? **Write them in the space below.**

_____

_____

_____

_____

_____

_____

_____

_____

_____

_____

What you just wrote separates you from God. Every sin does. And that feels bad, doesn't it?

Nancy

Eve could have easily believed that her sin was not that big of a deal. After all, she didn't divorce Adam; she didn't swear at God, or say He doesn't exist. All she did was take a bite of something God told her not to eat. What was the big deal? The big deal was that God said, "Don't," and Eve said, "I will."[2]

NOTES FOR MOM

Conversation Tip for Truth #10:

Ask your daughter to tell you about the last time she remembers acting sinfully. Then, ask her to recall what consequences she experienced. Maybe she felt like she was keeping a secret from you. Or perhaps she and her best friend weren't close for a while. Sin usually separates us from the people we know and love. Use that to help her understand how sad God is when she is separated from Him by her sin.

If you like being in a happy relationship with God and others, it's a good idea to do your best to avoid sinning. But, when you do sin—which we all do sometimes and is exactly why we need Jesus—here's another important Truth Nugget for you.

TRUTH NUGGET: "But if we confess our sins to him, he is faithful and just to forgive us our sins." (1 John 1:9)

Be quick to confess your sin. God is always ready to forgive you and welcome you back into friendship with Him. And, He'll even help you restore your friendships with others.

Speaking of others, do you want to know if I told my dad about the red juice? I'll tell you in the next section.

TRUTH #11 Hiding sin sets you up for failure.

A few weeks after I spilled the red juice and lied to my dad about it, my parents dropped me off at summer camp. I was so sure a week of pool time, the snack bar, and campfires would ease the guilt. I was wrong!

One night at a campfire, our counselor talked about sin and confession. The whole cabin started confessing really big sins. One girl said she had a secret boyfriend. Another one told us she had stolen something. And some shared even worse things.

Our counselor prayed with each girl, and then simply said to them, "I think you should call your parents."

There was **NOOOOO WAY** I was gonna tell my secret. **What if she made me tell my dad?**

Here's the thing. As we sat there in that room, I started to feel guilty. It was heavier than it had ever been. (My mom later told me that this feeling is called "conviction.") All this time, I had hoped I could wait the guilt out. But it just doesn't work that way. Guilt grows. It doesn't go away. I was miserable!

Suddenly, I couldn't stand it anymore.

"I did it! I spilled the red juice," I cried out.

The entire cabin stared at me wide-eyed. Yet no one made me feel like my sin was worse than theirs, or like it wasn't big enough to share. They just prayed with me. And then . . . my counselor said **IT**. The thing I dreaded most: **"I think you should call your dad."**

A lie I believed was quickly dying.

▶ LIE: "I DON'T NEED TO TELL ANYONE ABOUT MY SIN." ◀

WE ASKED 1,531 GIRLS IF THEY HAD ANY SECRETS ABOUT SIN.
More than half said they do have secrets about sin.

We asked them to explain what they meant.

🍎 Some said they had a secret about their own sin.

🍎 Some said they keep doing the same sin over and over again, but never talk to an adult to get help.

🍎 Some said they knew about someone else's sin and thought they should tell an adult, but felt afraid.

Maybe you too have believed that you don't need to tell anyone about your sin, or someone else's sin. There are a lot of lies that grow along with this one. Things like:

"No one needs to know about my sin in order for me to stop."

"It's always right to keep a secret."

"If I tell _____, they might not like or love me anymore."

NOTES FOR MOM

Conversation Tips for Truth #11:

Tell your daughter about a time when you confessed your sin to someone and it helped you experience freedom and grace. Then, invite her to do the same thing with you. Take your time with this simple assignment. It is a big one!

Some girls try to manage their sinful situation by hiding it. They want to overcome it, avoid disappointing their parents, or keep their friends from hating them. But here's the super sad reality: hiding your sin results in the exact opposite.

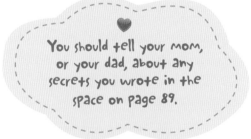

TRUTH NUGGET: "People who conceal their sins will not prosper, but if they confess and turn from them, they will receive mercy." (Proverbs 28:13)

It is natural to want to conceal, or hide, sin. Everyone does it. Since the beginning of time when Adam and Eve hid, people have been hiding their sin. But the Bible says you will not succeed if you **keep** hiding your sin.

Remember Gigi's lie about the slumber party? Just like Gigi's lie was meant to protect Zoey and didn't, hiding your sin isn't really protecting you. Rather, it's probably going to get you into trouble and make you feel lonely. Why? Because when you hide your sin, you can't get the help you need.

It is hard to learn from a poor decision or sin, until you admit that you did it and confess it. It is also hard to figure out how to stop sinning without some help. Everyone sins, but the Bible says only a fool keeps doing the same thing over and over again.

I'm going to tell you the thing you may not want to hear:

> You should tell your mom, or your dad, about any secrets you wrote in the space on page 89.

What you wrote in that box separates you from God if you have not confessed it to Him. And it might be getting in the way of your relationships with other people too. The Bible tells us to "confess your sins to each other" (James 5:16). Only God can forgive sins, but He wants us to confess to other people so we can get help.

It feels bad to hide your sin. You know what feels really great? Telling someone about your sin! It's one of the most freeing things I've ever done.

That night after the campfire, I called my dad. I told him what I had done, and asked for his forgiveness. He said, "Yeah, I know." The truth is he was way more disappointed that I was lying to him than he would have been if I had just confessed that I disobeyed him. And, he was really happy that I finally told him. He was just waiting for it, because he knew I would feel better. Telling my dad about my sin didn't make me feel worse. It made me feel better.

> **TRUTH #12**
> Everything we see or hear should be true, noble, right, pure, lovely, worthy of respect, excellent, and praiseworthy.

People spend a lot of money on entertainment. Movies. Music. The internet. Books. Apps. Because, well . . . they **entertain** us! But did you know that these things can also **change** us?

What we watch and listen to can change the way we think and how we behave, either in positive ways or negative ways depending on what we watch. Do you know why? Because it's kind of like "dwelling" on thoughts. (Remember that word from the beginning of the book?) When you think about something long enough, you could start believing it.

Be careful! You could give the control of your thoughts over to the entertainment world. It might be "normal" to watch and listen to anything you feel like, but remember: we must check our feelings with God's Truth. Let's do that now. ▼

TRUTH NUGGET: "And now, dear brothers and sisters, one final thing. Fix your thoughts on what is true, and honorable, and right, and pure, and lovely, and admirable. Think about things that are excellent and worthy of praise." (Philippians 4:8)

This verse gives us some simple tests for all the movies, TV shows, songs, podcasts, books, and pictures or stories we see on the internet. Think about the last movie, TV show, or song you watched or listened to and **write the name of it here:**

NOTES FOR MOM

Conversation Tips for Truth #12:

Take a moment to complete the challenge on this page. How do your media choices line up with this teaching? If you're telling your daughter one thing but living another, you will undermine any effort to train her to be wise and discerning about what she puts into her mind.

If your daughter has completed the challenging assignment for Truth #12 independently, ask her if she's willing to share her work. Praise her if she discerned wisely. Use questions to help her make a better choice, if she did not. Avoid giving her a black and white answer. Direct her to a wise decision using questions.

"What about that media was good and pure and lovely?"

"Can you give me an example of how what it presented is true?"

"Would you watch that movie (or listen to that song, or visit that website) with me or your dad?"

This task is a little more advanced. If your daughter didn't do it on her own, be prepared to take time and slowly work through the grid together. Encourage her to apply this Bible verse consistently to her entertainment choices.

NOW, LET'S RUN IT THROUGH THE TEST.

Check each box if the answer to the question is "yes."

☐ Is it true?
(There were *no* untruthful things in it, like teaching about evolution or saying that God is not real.)

☐ Is it noble?
(There were no scenes, lyrics, or situations that made bad things like drinking or drugs attractive.)

☐ Is it right?
(Your parents and teachers would say it was okay for you to see or listen to it.)

☐ Is it pure?
(People were dressed and speaking modestly.)

☐ Is it lovely?
(It did not leave you with ugly or violent thoughts or pictures.)

☐ Is it worthy of respect?
(You would show it to your parents, your pastor, your teachers, and others.)

☐ Is it excellent?
(It was created with care, and helped you use your imagination.)

☐ Is it praiseworthy?
(You would recommend it to others.)

How did your movie, TV show, or song do? It had to get a checkmark on **EACH QUALITY** to be something God would really want you to watch. Otherwise, it's **possible** it was either sinful to watch or it is training your mind for sinfulness. It's that simple.

Even so, some girls still believe this lie.

▶ LIE: "WHAT I WATCH/LISTEN TO DOESN'T MATTER." ◀

Are you one of them? If you are, let me encourage you to talk to your mom or dad today. Tell them that you feel that God is asking you to be more careful about your entertainment choices and you'd like some help. I bet they'd be really happy you asked!

NOTES FOR MOM

Since the assignments for your daughter's lab work are the same regardless of the chapter content, I only provided ideas about how to interact with your daughter at the end of chapter 4. You can refer back to those "Notes for Mom" on pages 72–73 if you need a refresher.

YOUR TURN IN THE LAB

Grab your pencils. It's your turn to do some work in our Truth Lab.

THE LIE

THE TRUTH

Sin isn't that big of a deal.

• Sin separates us from God, no matter how big or small. (Isaiah 59:2)

• If we confess our sin, God will forgive us. (1 John 1:9)

I don't need to tell anyone about my sin.

• Hiding your sin feels really bad.

• You cannot overcome your sin and learn from it, if you don't get advice. (Proverbs 28:13)

• The Bible tells you to confess your sins to someone. (James 5:16)

• Only God can forgive you, but He is always faithful and fair and will forgive us when we confess to Him. (1 John 1:9)

What I watch/listen to doesn't matter.

• Everything we see or hear should be true, noble, right, pure, lovely, worthy of respect, excellent, and praiseworthy. (Philippians 4:8)

THINKING ABOUT TRUTH

TELLING MYSELF THE TRUTH
It's your turn to be the author!

💜 Have you believed any of these lies about sin? Put an X on top of any of **THE LIES** in this chapter that you have believed.

💜 What Truth do you need to think about **all the time**, EVERY DAY? Look at **THE TRUTH** we dug up together. Now circle what seems important for you personally to dwell on.

💜 Next, begin to think about it **all the time**, EVERY DAY. You can start by writing a prayer to God, a helpful Bible verse, or some ideas you don't want to forget in the space below.

Helping Zoey Believe Truth
It's time to give Zoey some advice!

What do you think? Should Zoey have a sleepover, and *not* invite Gigi? Why?

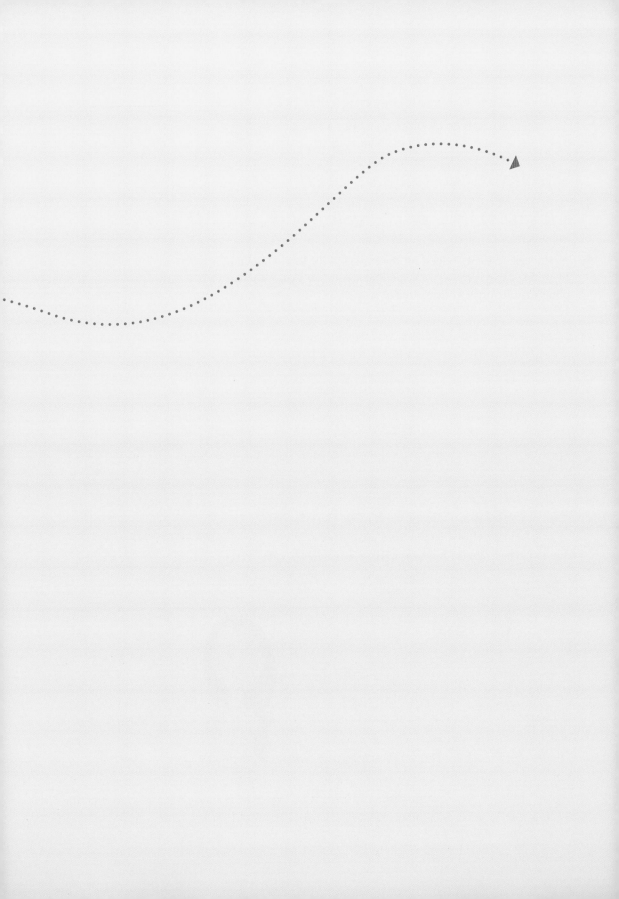

Truth and Lies about Being a Girl

The first words the girls who took our survey read were these: *"To take this survey, you have to be a girl between the ages of 7–12. How do you feel about being a girl?"*

- 48% chose "It's great to be a girl."

- 46% chose "Sometimes it's hard, but I usually enjoy being a girl."

- 1% chose "I don't like being a girl."

- 4% chose "I don't think there is any difference between boys and girls."*

Some of the respondents who didn't like being a girl left comments like these.

- *I'm aware that girls are treated and perceived differently than boys, even though girls can accomplish anything.*

- *It's harder than being a boy.*

- *I want to be strong like a boy.*

Since I've never felt this way, I sought out a handful of my adult female friends who once did. My goal was to understand the feelings they—and ultimately these girls—have experienced. My friends' reasons ranged from the desire to explore opportunities men have, to wishing they could use their athletic abilities to compete with boys. Each of my friends successfully navigated their angst, and today enjoys being female.

It was once assumed that a girl's dissonance with her gender was something that eventually passed. That is no longer true. A recent article in *The Atlantic* reports on the accelerated process of transitioning for transgender children.[1] (The term *transgender* is used to describe an individual whose sense of gender does not correspond with his or her biological sex.)

* The remaining percentage of girls selected "other" because none of the statements reflected how they felt about being a girl.

However, research and experience seem to indicate that many children experience gender nonconformity of some type. A girl may like to play with trucks, or hunt with her dad. Or a boy may love the color pink, or gardening with his mom. These desires don't fit into cultural stereotypes. Even so, most children who experience them grow up to be comfortable with their biological sex. Rushing to change the bodies of children struggling with their gender risks causing great—sometimes irreparable—damage.

The author of *The Atlantic* article shares the story of a girl identified as Claire. Depression arrived with puberty. She became uncomfortable in her body and didn't like being a girl.

Claire started watching YouTube videos made by transgender young people. She began to wonder if she was uncomfortable with her body because she was really male, and began to believe she was supposed to be a boy. She began to dress and act like one. Eventually, Claire asked her parents for "top surgery"—a double mastectomy—and testosterone. A licensed therapist suggested it was a good idea and referred the family to a clinic.

But Claire's mom and dad weren't so sure. They lovingly encouraged their daughter to explore her feelings further and suggested journaling. To some, this would appear unkind and nonaffirming.

Claire decided to indulge her parents. One day when writing an entry, she concluded that after living as a boy and looking like one, *she still wasn't happy.* This caused her to realize she was not male, after all. Following more thoughtful consideration, she discovered that her unhappiness with being a girl stemmed from rigid beliefs she had developed about gender. When the unhealthy stereotypes were addressed, she felt permission to be herself. Today she feels at home in her body and is happy to be a girl.

What would have happened if Claire's parents had followed through on the counselor's advice to help their daughter transition?

Culture is eager to redefine gender. Friends, media, and even well-meaning therapists invite developing minds to question whether their gender matches their biological sex. What are you doing to prepare your daughter to believe Truth in the midst of this cultural conversation that is taking place on every front?

You cannot always depend on the church at large to model a healthy way to respond. Often, we have been guilty of entering the public discourse with either painful accusation, or heartfelt but misguided affirmation.

We must prepare our children to respond with convictional kindness. They need a conviction to believe what God's Word teaches about gender. But they must learn to express these beliefs with kindness.

To learn this skill, let's examine the example of Jesus. When He walked this earth, people sought affirmation from the religious world to redefine the covenant of marriage. They wanted to marry and divorce at will. Some Pharisees asked Jesus about it, but it was a trap. They hoped His answer would cause Him to lose the respect of the masses. Below is one account of that interaction. (I've underlined some words so you can take special note of them.) ▶

TRUTH NUGGET: "Some Pharisees came and tried to trap [Jesus] with this question: 'Should a man be allowed to divorce his wife for just any reason?'

'Haven't you read the Scriptures?' Jesus replied. 'They record that from the beginning "God made them male and female."' And he said, "'This explains why a man leaves his father and mother and is joined to his wife, and the two are united into one." Since they are no longer two but one, let no one split apart what God has joined together.'

'Then why did Moses say in the law that a man could give his wife a written notice of divorce and send her away?' they asked.

Jesus replied, 'Moses permitted divorce only as a concession to your hard hearts, but it was not <u>what God had originally intended</u>.'"
(Matthew 19:3–8)

When confronted with a sensitive cultural conversation, Jesus pointed back to creation to affirm and explain what God originally intended when He designed marriage and biological sex. He said "from the beginning" "God had originally intended" a male and a female to come together in marriage and when they did, He would make them one. Jesus affirmed Truth by pointing His listeners back to Genesis.

This is a wise example for us to follow as we face questions about gender. We must root what we believe about sex, sexuality, and marriage in God's original intentions. He created us. He knows—better than we do—how our bodies, minds, and spirits work. A pastor I know puts it this way:

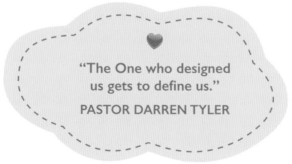

"The One who designed us gets to define us."
PASTOR DARREN TYLER

In the beginning, God *chose* to make us male and female. And like most artists, His creative choice has meaning. Within the design is a picture of Himself.

 TRUTH NUGGET: "So God created human beings in his own image. In the image of God he created them; male and female he created them." (Genesis 1:27)

Embracing our femaleness—as men embrace their maleness—somehow enables a lost world to see God. Many things about us reflect His image. We are intelligent, worshipful, and creative. We have defied gravity to fly spaceships to the moon and unlocked languages to communicate with one another. Why doesn't the Bible reference such traits when conveying that we reflect

His image? It mentions only our maleness and femaleness. These two binary genders are an essential part of looking like Him.

Why? Well, one reason may be that it displays a unique aspect of the social nature of the Trinity. God the Father, God the Son, and God the Holy Spirit are distinctly different, and yet they are one. In the Old Testament, the word for God's oneness is *echad* (see Deuteronomy 6:4).

Male and female come together in marriage and also become one. The Bible uses the same word—*echad*—to describe the union of one man and one woman in marriage (Genesis 2:24). In this way, gender helps to complete the picture of looking like God.

This Truth is critical.

Of course, it doesn't erase the pain and complexities of children and adults living through the confusion of not identifying with their biological sex. Gender dysphoria is real.

So is intersexuality, which is a term used for a number of different conditions, often involving a chromosomal abnormality, in which someone is born with a reproductive or sexual anatomy that is not clearly male or female. In such cases, a sex development specialist is brought in to consult. Blood tests generally reveal that the baby is biologically male or female. But in some extremely rare situations, no clear sex is evident.

Such was the case of "Laurie," whose adoptive mom called me seeking answers. What her mom told me about the Christian community broke my heart.

"You are the first Christian person who has been willing to dialogue with us," she said. "This topic is just too difficult for those who want everything to be black and white."

For now, Laurie's parents are raising their child as a girl. Answers are elusive, so they are not pursuing any sex-assignment surgeries. They will help Laurie make those decisions as she grows up.

Rare and complex cases such as this one are often used to legitimize transgenderism. However, intersexuality is a physiological condition, whereas gender dysphoria is a psychological condition.

Chromosomal abnormalities are a reality in our broken, fallen world. These include things like Down Syndrome or Klinefelter Syndrome (where a male has an extra X chromosome resulting in language and fertility challenges) or Fragile X Syndrome (a common cause of autism). Syndromes are a painful biological fact that must be addressed with love and compassion.

Mental disorders and distresses are another reality in this world. Some of these are sexual in nature, or related to gender. These conditions are often accompanied by PTSD, suicidal tendencies, depression, and other difficulties, which generally do not go away after sex reassignment surgeries have been completed.[2] How can our hearts not break for those afflicted by these disorders?

If your daughter struggles with such pain, I pray you will find a loving Christian community to help you. If your daughter doesn't face gender confusion, may she become a source of compassion.

Please understand that compassion does not displace conviction. We can trust the Bible to answer our questions about the body, sexuality, and gender. But we live in a fallen world where we need to equip our children with conviction marked by compassion.

TALKING WITH GOD:

Use Genesis 1:27 to write a prayer asking God to help your daughter embrace being a girl. Ask Him to give her a heart to reflect His image. Write out your prayer in the lines below.

So God created human beings in his own image.
In the image of God he created them;
male and female he created them.
(Genesis 1:27)

_____

_____

_____

_____

_____

TALKING WITH YOUR GIRL:

Now that you've prayed, invite your daughter to read chapter 8 in her book while you review the same content right here. I've written a few notes for you in the margins. You might want to add some of your own to help prompt you when it's time to discuss this chapter with your girl.

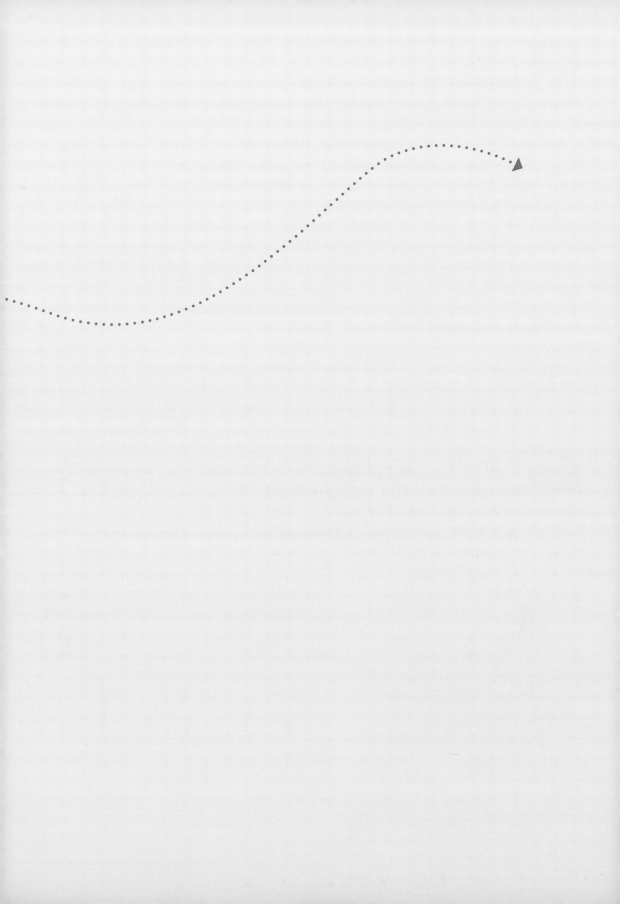

Lies about Being a Girl

CHAPTER 8

"It's GREAT to be a girl!"

I shouted that today at recess when Gigi, Via, and I were going as fast as we could on the merry-go-round. Every day we try to see who can stay on the longest. It was **ME** today. Via gave up real quick, and Gigi went down next. We were laying on the ground, trying not to puke, when Via shouted, **"Girls RULE. Boys DROOOOL!"** Gigi said her mom doesn't let her say that because girls and boys are both important. That made Via mad. She asked Gigi, "Are you a girl hater?" Gigi said, "No! But why do you think boys have to be stupid for girls to feel smart?" Then, they had a big conversation that didn't make a lot of sense to me. They both say girls and boys aren't different, but how can Via say that AND believe "Girls Rule. Boys Drool"? SIGH! I'm super confused.

Doodle your heart out here, Mom! This is your notepad!

You aren't the only one, Zoey. It seems everyone, everywhere is talking about "Girls Rule. Boys Drool." They may not use those exact words, but they are trying to figure out if girls or boys are more important. Some are even trying to get rid of the differences between boys and girls.

Sometimes there are differences that are not good, and need to be changed. When I was a girl, many women did the same kind of work as men but got paid less than men. Now people have realized that's not okay, and are fighting to change things so men and women who have the same jobs and experience get paid the same. That's a good thing!

But sometimes the way people try to erase differences is not okay. While it is okay for a girl to dress more like a tomboy than a princess, she should also think, "It's great to be a girl." That doesn't mean she can't play basketball or work in construction, or that she can't like *Star Wars* more than *Cinderella*. It means that a girl shouldn't want to be so much like a boy that it erases everything about her that makes her girl-like. Doing that sends the message that being a girl isn't great at all.

Let's get right to an important Truth that you need to know about being a girl.

TRUTH #13

God created two different genders: male & female.

From the moment you were born (and even before that, according to Psalm 139:13–16), you were different from every boy ever born. Some things are obvious, but females and males are different in ways that you might not even see.

GIRLS & WOMEN

The bodies of most teen girls turn energy into a thicker layer of body fat, which gives them the ability to cushion and protect a baby one day. (This also makes them better at swim competitions, because their body stays warmer and works better in the water!)

Adult women have wider pelvis openings (which means their hips are more spread out and looser), giving them the ability to have babies in the future.

Women's brains tend to have more "wires" that connect thoughts, giving them the ability to do a lot of things at one time.

BOYS & MEN

The bodies of most teen boys turn energy into lean muscle, and by age 18, have 50% more muscle than most girls. This gives them more strength, and the ability to do harder physical work than most girls their age.[3]

Adult men have more compact pelvis structures (which means their hips are more tightly constructed and stronger). This gives them the ability to carry heavy things for longer periods of time without hurting themselves.[4]

Men's brains tend to have fewer and more direct "wires" to connect thoughts, giving them the ability to focus on one thing and be slow, thorough problem-solvers.[5]

NOTES FOR MOM

About Truth #13:

Just as God spoke to Adam about the forbidden tree in the garden without exposing him to sin, you can have a conversation with your daughter about gender and sexuality that is pure and appropriate. This chapter has been carefully vetted by numerous mothers to present Truth without robbing your girl of innocence.

It is not unlikely that your daughter has already encountered some of the lies about gender and sexuality embedded in our world. Be prepared to talk openly about them as you navigate this conversation. It's better that you answer her questions than for her curiosity to lead her to friends or the internet.

While this chapter is not about sex, it's possible that it will prompt a conversation about it. See the next chapter's introduction for some important information about "the talk."

NOTES FOR MOM

Conversation Tip for Truth #13:

Ask your daughter how she feels about being a girl. Be willing to have an open discussion about things she doesn't like.

Then, explore whether or not she knows anyone who is a girl, but doesn't like it. This question is a safe way to discover how much she has been exposed to regarding gender confusion. Perhaps she has a friend who is a great athlete and wishes she could play boys' soccer. This innocent developmental phase is easy to talk about. But she also may know of a classmate, neighbor, or friend who is transitioning with the help of parents and professionals. Be prepared to discuss this. This chapter offers only a brief overview on a difficult topic. If you don't feel ready for the conversation, research biblical Truth about gender.

Of course, there are still exceptions to everything in that chart. You just need to be the kind of girl God created you to be!

The point I'm making is this: It's true that girls and boys **can** both do **almost** anything. But their bodies, brains, and strengths generally have the word "different" written all over them.

Even so, a lot of people today believe this lie.

▶ **LIE: "BOYS AND GIRLS AREN'T REALLY THAT DIFFERENT."** ◀

Sometimes girls feel this way because they **do** like basketball or construction or *Star Wars*. Maybe they even want to "be strong like boys." (It's okay to work out and grow stronger, if that's something that's important to you.) Sometimes girls feel this way because they want to play football with their brothers or hunt with their dads. (It's okay to get out there and try things some other girls aren't doing!) Sometimes girls feel this way because they don't like the color pink or wearing dresses. (It's okay to love the color blue, and like wearing pants!) It's okay to be a different kind of girl.

But sometimes girls think boys and girls aren't different because they feel confused when someone they know is born a girl but **REALLY** wishes they were a boy. Is that okay? Let's look at a Bible verse to find an answer. ▼

 **TRUTH NUGGET:** "Then God said, 'Let us make human beings in our image, to be like us. . . .' So God created human beings in his own image. In the image of God he created them; male and female he created them." (Genesis 1:26—27)

You were created in God's "likeness." That means you were created to make people remember and think about God, because there are things about you that are like Him. **HOW COOL IS THAT?**

Grab two pencils. Circle the two words in our Truth Nugget that tell us what two specific things are mentioned about how we were created. I hope you circled the words **male** and **female**. Of course, there are a lot of things that make us like God. Our brains. Our creativity. But God only mentions **male** and **female** in this verse. So, being a girl must be a big deal. (So is being a boy. That's why I don't really like sayings like, "Girls rule! Boys drool!")

NOTES FOR MOM

Big Question:

Is it more effective to win people to Christ by proving we're right about complicated social issues, or by loving people well?

But **WHY** did God create different sexes, or genders?

It's because He wants us to look like Him. You might be wondering:

How does being a girl or a boy help us do THAT?

I'm glad you asked!

God is three different persons, who are really **ONE**. God the Father, God the Son, and God the Holy Spirit make up what's called the Trinity. ▶

When He created us as **male** and **female**, He gave us the ability to be two completely different people who could be joined by God, through marriage, into **ONE**.

Does that mean you **have** to get married? No! But God created two genders. Male. Female. And it's important that you help to protect that Truth.

It's also important to say that you believe God created differences in females and males. This includes learning what the Bible teaches us about how we should interact with each other. It is important to know God's guidelines about how men and women were created so that we can live in this world the way that God planned.

This is one lie where the Bible chimes in loud and clear. It tells us that when someone decides to make up their own truth about males and females, they have "traded the truth about God for a lie" (Romans 1:25).

▶ **CHOOSE TRUTH!** ◀

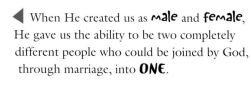

NOTES FOR MOM

About Truth #14:

Many girls get their periods without ever being taught about it. That can be frightening. Girls reach menarche—the first occurrence of menstruation—as young as nine, so it's a good idea to cover this topic before then.

Getting her period is a beautiful sign that your daughter's body is preparing to make new life. Use this chapter to set the stage to tell her how everything works, or to continue the conversation.

If you are unsure how to know that she is ready, breast buds generally appear six months to one year before a girl's first period. But sometimes even these don't signal you to have the conversation. It's better to get ahead of her experience with practical advice, so she is prepared for this landmark in her life.

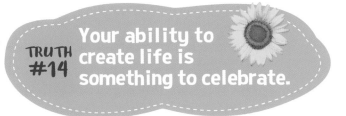

TRUTH #14 Your ability to create life is something to celebrate.

No one hands out awards, but every girl is going to change into a woman. This includes you! One of the biggest changes is getting your period. It happens anywhere between the ages of 9 and 16, so it's kinda hard to know exactly when it'll happen. The most noticeable sign will be some blood in your underwear. **Don't worry!** It's not because you're hurt, and it's totally normal. (Your mom, or grandma, or an auntie will help you learn more about how to take care of your body.)

Let me tell you what's really happening when you get your period. You have about 300,000 eggs in your body right now that could each become a full-out **HUMAN BEING**! (Relax! You're not going to have 300,000 babies.) Here's how it works:

- Each month some of these eggs are released from the part of your body called ovaries.

- A triangle shaped area called the uterus builds a nice, soft, cushiony lining so that **if** one or two of those eggs happens to begin to become a baby, there is a safe place to grow.

- But, if that doesn't happen, the uterus sheds its soft, cushy lining. This is what you see when you see blood.

WHAT IT LOOKS LIKE INSIDE YOUR BODY

Your period is all very scientific and amazing. The coolest thing is it reminds you that you are uniquely designed as a girl, and one of the special abilities of being female is the **POSSIBILITY** of having babies one day. Here's what God says about becoming a mom: ▼

 TRUTH NUGGET: "Children are a gift from the Lord; they are a reward from him." (Psalm 127:3)

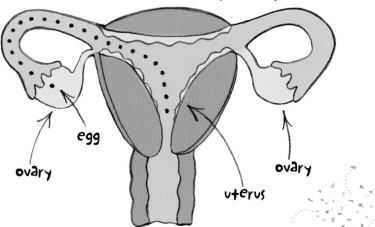

what it looks like inside your body

egg

ovary

ovary

uterus

Having a body that is able to create babies is a good reason to celebrate! Some girls do something special when they start their period. Their moms take them out for a special dinner, or have a party where other women give them advice. I think that's a good idea.

But not everyone thinks getting their period is something to celebrate.

Some girls (and even some moms) believe this lie.

▶ LIE: "GETTING MY PERIOD IS GOING TO BE AWFUL." ◀

It is true that getting your period can be uncomfortable. Sometimes you have tummy cramps, or a headache. Some girls even get super moody and mean. (Don't do that! Having your period is not an excuse to be mean.) It's also true that having babies hurts. It is also wonderfully true that you generally forget the pain.

Trust me, getting your period is probably not going to be nearly as bad as you think. It's just new.

Something that has helped me respond well to my period is remembering that God wants us to do "everything" without "complaining." That includes getting your period. Remember that verse from Truth #6?

First Thessalonians 5:18 says "in everything give thanks" (NKJV). I find that anything hard becomes easier when I am thankful. Why not try telling God thanks for making you a girl instead of being nervous about your period? It's coming one way or another. You might as well have a good attitude about it.

Instead of dreading your period, kick off your womanhood with some celebration. It's not awful. It's actually awesome proof of your God-designed ability to have a baby, and it's worth celebrating.

NOTES FOR MOM

Conversation Tips for Truth #14:

Be sure to present this topic positively. Many of the seven to twelve-year-old girls who took our survey expressed some strong fears about both their changing bodies and eventually having babies. Your first conversation about your daughter's period frames the way she thinks about the process of becoming a mom. I can't think of anything more wonderful for her future than the possibility of giving birth.

You'll note that I included the word *possibility* (which I have highlighted for you) in your daughter's book when I wrote about having babies. That's because sometimes, God provides babies through adoption. (One of my two girls is adopted.) And sometimes, His plan for a woman's life does not include children at all. Be sure to direct your conversation to prepare her for these possibilities, as well.

NOTES FOR MOM

Since the assignments for your daughter's lab work are the same regardless of the chapter content, I only provided ideas about how to interact with your daughter at the end of chapter 4. You can refer back to those "Notes for Mom" on pages 72–73 if you need a refresher.

YOUR TURN IN THE TRUTH LAB

Grab your pencils. It's your turn to dig deep.

THE LIE

Boys and girls aren't really different.

THE TRUTH

• **God created two different genders: male and female.** (Genesis 1:27)

• **Girls and boys have a lot of physical, mental, and practical differences.**

• **It's okay to be a different kind of girl, as long as you believe God made you to be a girl.**

• **Those who do not believe in only two distinct genders—male and female— have traded God's Truth for a lie.** (Romans 1:25)

Getting my period is going to be awful.

• **Your period is awesome proof of your God-designed ability to have babies, and worth celebrating.**

• **Having babies is a gift from God.** (Psalm 127:3, 5a)

• **You should do everything—including getting your period—without grumbling or complaining.** (Philippians 2:14,16)

• **You should do everything—including getting your period—with thanksgiving to God.** (1 Thessalonians 5:18)

THINKING ABOUT TRUTH

TELLING MYSELF THE TRUTH

It's your turn to be the author!

🩶 Have you believed any of these lies about being a girl? Put an X on top of any of **THE LIES** in this chapter that you have believed.

🩶 What Truth do you need to think about **all the time**, **EVERY DAY**? Look at **THE TRUTH** we dug up together. Now circle what seems important for you personally to dwell on.

🩶 Next, begin to think about it **all the time**, **EVERY DAY**. You can start by writing a prayer to God, a helpful Bible verse, or some ideas you don't want to forget in the space below.

Helping Zoey Believe Truth
It's time to give Zoey some advice!

The conversation Zoey overheard at recess revealed that her friends are confused about the differences between boys and girls. Zoey got confused, too. Do you think it was okay for her friend to say, "Girls rule. Boys drool"? Why or why not?

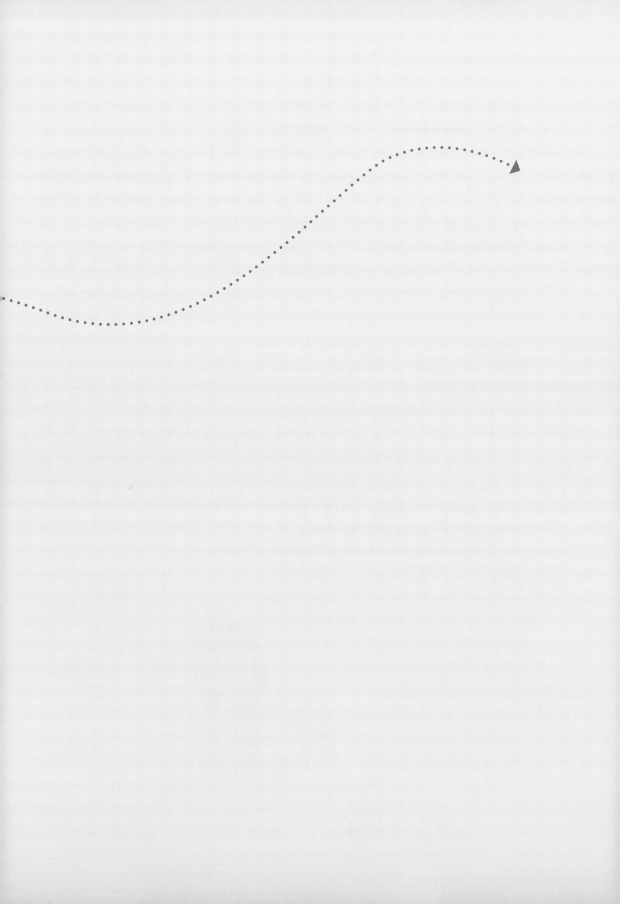

Truth and Lies about Boys

You might think it's natural to talk to your daughter about boys. Or maybe you avoid it like the plague. Either way, it's essential, and you probably know that.

The focus groups I conducted with mothers revealed that the topic of "boys/sex" was third on the list of lies that most concerned them. Many moms had regrets from their teen years, which they hoped their daughter would not experience. Others were just overwhelmed by boy craziness and sexual messages in the culture. But most of them knew that planting seeds of Truth on the topics of boys and sex mattered.

When I began to talk to their daughters, I quickly identified a significant barrier hindering conversation. The most common statement I heard from girls as we explored the topic was: *"Talking to my mom about boys is 'weird'!"*

There were multiple reasons they felt uncomfortable talking to their moms about boys, but one of their concerns, in particular, weighs heavy on my heart. Girls feared that their moms would tell other people their private thoughts and feelings, or recount stories that would make people laugh at them. One girl put it this way:

I don't talk to my mom about boys because it might spread to lots of people.

One of the crucial aspects of teaching your child biblical Truth about boys and sex is keeping the lines of communication open. Nothing will shut her down faster than feeling embarrassed or that her trust was betrayed. (You might consider that the next time you post a photo of her or a story about her on social media.)

A Bible verse that keeps me careful with what I say about my children is directed at fathers. But I think the principle is also valuable for us as mothers. ▼

 TRUTH NUGGET: "Fathers, do not aggravate your children, or they will become discouraged." (Colossians 3:21)

As parents, sometimes our actions can frustrate our children, causing them to feel angry, bitter, and discouraged. Here are a few things that may help you avoid aggravating your daughter when the topics of boys and sex come up.

1 **Your daughter may unwittingly say something inaccurate** or amusing as you discuss boys and sex. Don't make her feel like the laughing stock. Instead, create a safe space for her to make innocent mistakes. This builds trust so that she continues to explore sometimes-awkward topics with you. In all honesty, this is something I wish I had done better with my girls.

2 **You will need advice sometimes** to respond to your daughter's questions and experiences. Seek it discreetly from sources that protect her privacy. There will be times when you need to seek help. Be wise in how you go about getting it. Let your girl know ahead of time that you plan to ask someone for advice about her situation. Say something like: *"I don't know how to help you with this, but _____ has been a great source of wisdom for me when I have private problems. Would you mind if I asked her what she thinks?"* Disclosing your intentions up front generally builds trust, rather than breaking it when she finds out about it after the fact.

3 **As you build trust with your daughter,** she may tell you about the behaviors of her friends which you will need to report to another adult. Let your girl know she can talk to you about anything. However, if you become aware that someone is involved in unhealthy or dangerous behaviors, it is your responsibility to help. Telling her this will usually open the lines of communication rather than stifle them. She will see that a primary motivation is protection.

Another barrier to healthy conversations with your daughter about boys and sex is pain from the past. I'm talking about your past. And mine.

If we want to effectively help our daughters develop a healthy view of boys and sex, we need to have one ourselves. I encourage you to pursue healing. For me, this required professional Christian counseling, wise advice from older women, and lots of time with Jesus. I had to do some hard work to overcome the lies that become embedded in my heart as a result of my foolish decisions. Your wholeness builds a foundation for you to teach your daughter Truth about boys and sex.

Yes, talking about boys means you also have to talk about sex.

Most children are developmentally ready for this topic during their ninth year. Around this age, I encourage you to initiate this conversation so you can plant seeds of Truth and begin an ongoing discussion to form a healthy sexual ethic. In our focus groups, only about 50 percent of mothers with daughters who were nine or older, had talked to their girls about sex. Your silence creates a vacuum for the world's lies to enter in. Be the expert. Plant Truth.

This book is not meant to be a comprehensive guide for you as you talk to your daughter about sex. However, these conversation starters, grouped by developmental stage, may help. I hope they give you courage and a starting point.

CONVERSATION STARTERS FOR EACH STAGE OF MORAL DEVELOPMENT

Copycat
(Ages 2-5)

"It's great to be a girl."

"Boys and girls are different."

"There are good pictures and bad pictures on the internet. Some of the bad pictures contain people without clothes on. If you ever see a bad picture, you should tell me. Okay?" *(This is an important conversation to protect your child from pornography.)*

Counseling
(Ages 6-11)

"Our family preference for when you can start to date is _____. We hope you will choose to wait until then to have a boyfriend."

"Your dad and I would like to be the ones to answer your questions about boys. How can we make that comfortable for you?"

"God created the private body part of a man (which is called a penis) to fit into the private body part of a woman (which is called a vagina). Sometimes when a husband and wife want to show each other how much they love one another, they put those parts together. We call that sex."

"Sex is a wonderful gift from God for a man and woman to share together when they are married."

Coaching
(Ages 12+)

"Your dad and I would like to be the one to answer your questions about sex and sexuality. How can we make that comfortable for you?"

"Having sex is not the only thing that is sexy or sexual. There are a lot of other things that lead up to it, so let's talk about what kind of boundaries you want to have before you are married." *(This conversation should include things like pornography, sexting, mastur-bation, oral sex, "making out," "hooking up," etc.)*

You and your daughter *can* get to a point where you both acknowledge the tension surrounding the conversation, but also feel good about having it. One of the tween girls I talked to put it this way:

It's weird to talk to my mom about boys but after you do you feel a lot better.

TALKING WITH GOD:

Use Colossians 3:21 to write an honest prayer to God. If you have felt convicted by anything I have written in this chapter, confess it to God. If you have not, ask Him to reveal to you any way that you may be aggravating or discouraging your daughter. Write out your prayer in the lines below.

Fathers, do not aggravate your children,
or they will become discouraged.
(Colossians 3:21)

_____

_____

_____

_____

_____

TALKING WITH YOUR GIRL:

Now that you've prayed, invite your daughter to read chapter 9 in her book while you review the same content right here. I've written a few notes for you in the margins. You might want to add some of your own to help prompt you when it's time to discuss this chapter with your girl.

Lies about Boys

CHAPTER
9

Doodle your heart out here, Mom! This is your notepad!

In the history of forever, I have never made it through a trip to my Grandma Bing's house without **The QUESTION!** At Christmas this year, I thought I was going to get through, but **NO.** We actually had our coats on, and our Christmas bags all packed up. My lil' bro was even in his car seat. I hugged Grandma Bing, and then it happened: **"So, do you have a boyfriend yet?"** I slipped into the minivan as fast as I could, and I jumped into the back seat, managing not to explode from embarrassment. **Good grief!** She's been asking me that since **KINDERGARTEN!!!**

Has that ever happened to you? Sometimes it's not just kids your age who pressure you into being boy crazy. It seems some of the most trusted adults think it's funny to ask girls if they have a boyfriend.

NOTES FOR MOM

Big Question:

Ephesians 5:31–32 teaches us that marriage is a picture of Christ and His bride, the church. If that is true, how motivated do you think Satan is to see that picture destroyed in your daughter's life?

About Truth #15:

Positive parenting messages are far more potent than negative ones. As you discuss this lie, I encourage you to tell your daughter *when* she may pursue her interest in boys.

I have had many conversations with heartbroken mothers who discovered that their sixth, seventh, or eighth-grade daughter had a boyfriend. I always ask them if they had previously communicated to her when she *could* have such a relationship. Sometimes they convey regret as they realize they missed an important window for this conversation.

Bob and I began to share our family preference for dating when our children were in early elementary school. Because we witnessed childish, but nonetheless real, "relationships" between kids starting in fourth or fifth grade, we wanted to get ahead of the culture on this one.

You cannot deny that girls and boys will experience attraction. Encourage your girl to respond to her

If you don't think it's funny, you've come to the right place. I don't think it's funny either. Liking boys is serious business, because **LIKING BOYS** usually leads to wanting to be in special relationships with them. **Being in special relationships with BOYS** usually leads to dating them. And **DATING BOYS** usually leads to marrying one. Most people think marriage is pretty serious, so I think the topic of boys is pretty serious, too.

Here's a truth that a lot of you already know, because over half of the girls we talked to told us, "I plan to wait until I'm older to have a boyfriend."

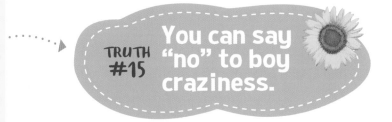

TRUTH #15

You can say "no" to boy craziness.

Maybe that sounds difficult to you. Even though a lot of girls didn't want to have a boyfriend yet, some of them already had one. So, I know you may feel some pressure.

You may even feel like you can't control the boy-crazy feelings you have. Maybe you believe that they're just feelings that naturally show up. Reminder: anytime you have a strong feeling, you need to check in with God's Truth to see how to respond to it. Here's a Truth Nugget that I hope will get some of you to jump off the boy-crazy train! ▼

TRUTH NUGGET: "Promise me . . . not to awaken love until the time is right." (Song of Solomon 2:7)

This verse is from the Bible's celebration of marriage and romantic love: Song of Solomon. The book says that both marriage and romance are good. It also gives helpful advice on how to experience love.

God designed marriage and love. He knows that feelings can overpower good choices, and that feelings aren't enough to support a relationship. This verse tells people of all ages not to get into a romantic relationship too soon, because it could grow faster than the commitment needed to make love last.

Are you ready to commit to someone for a lifetime? If the answer is no, this Bible verse applies to you. It's not the right time to "stir up" romantic love by being boy crazy.

Does that sound impossible in this boy-crazy world? God would not have put this verse in the Bible if it were **IMPOSSIBLE**! So, I know that you're able to say "no" to boy craziness. You may need to rely on God and others to help you, but it is possible.

Even so, some girls fall for this lie.

▶ LIE: "IT'S OKAY TO BE BOY CRAZY." ◀

21% of girls said it is okay to be boy crazy.

They told me it is "normal" to be boy crazy. Okay! Let me remind you once again: **normal is overrated!**

It's "normal" for some of your friends to be crazy about clothes and beauty products. But I can't find one place in the Bible where it says girls should be fashionable. I do find verses that say we should not be too concerned about those things.

It's "normal" for girls of all ages to have "frenemies"—friends who turn into enemies sometimes. And some say it's "normal" to be "mean girls." I can't find one place in the Bible where that's okay. Instead, I find verses that say things like this: **"Be kind to one another"** (Ephesians 4:32 NKJV).

It may also be "normal" for tween girls to be boy crazy, but it is not God's best. His word says you can wait, so I believe you're able to do that.

Do you know what kind of crazy you can be? God crazy! A God-crazy girl can be easily identified. She lets God have the first and last say in everything she does. That is to say, she obeys Him. Why not jump onto the God-crazy girl train with girls who believe, along with me, that they are able to wait for the right time to think about boys and love.

TRUTH #16 You will never outgrow the need for wise advice.

One way you can avoid being boy crazy is to talk to your mom. Or, she could help you jump off the boy-crazy train, if you're already on it. God gave you a mom to guide you. And the Bible says our parents should be the primary source of wisdom in all areas, including boys.

feelings by learning how to interact with guys as friends. After all, so much of marriage is friendship. It will be a great building block for her future, and will avoid her going along with the mindless boy-crazy crowd.

Conversation Tip for Truth #15:

If your daughter or her friends are boy crazy, this conversation may have a life of its own. Soak it in prayer, and go for it.

But maybe your daughter is a part of the 53 percent of tween girls who took my survey and said, "I'm not thinking about boys much." That's fantastic! This conversation will be brief, unless you use it to bridge to a broader topic: "normal is overrated."

You will notice that I often bring up this idea. *Normal* cannot be our measuring stick for Truth. God's Word gets that honor. Before you begin this conversation with your daughter, consider any areas where she may believe the lie that a behavior or activity is okay because it is "normal." Make a note of that, and focus your discussion where she needs it most.

NOTES FOR MOM

About Truth #16:

I truly hope that the conversation you and your daughter are about to have removes barriers from discussing boys and sex. Because your daughter—and you—will never outgrow the need for wise advice.

Do *you* need counsel about men and sex? Maybe you are a single mom and need to invite a godly, older woman into your life to help you approach your desires with wisdom and self-control.

Or maybe you are a married woman who is experiencing sexual barriers and needs to pursue professional Christian counseling so you can know the fullest extent of intimacy with your husband.

Seeking accountability and advice for yourself builds a foundation upon which to challenge your girl to do the same. I have found that it's tough to teach my daughters what I am not living out in my own life.

But this is where we have a super, ginormous, big problem to fix in the girl world.

80% of girls don't talk to their moms about boys.

Many of them say the reason is because it's weird.

Those girls are believing this lie.

▶ **LIE: "I DON'T NEED TO TALK TO MY MOM ABOUT BOYS."** ◀

GIRLS WHO BELIEVE THIS LIE SAID THINGS LIKE THIS:

 I'm not exactly comfortable talking about it with her.

It's my personal secret. It's personal!

It may feel "weird." You might feel like you'll be losing some of your freedom and independence. (Remember, you **don't** need freedom. See page 69.) Maybe you have some fears that your mom might talk to other people about what you say, like maybe your dad. (Let me encourage you to talk to your mom about THAT, so she can understand your perspective.)

Once again, you need to check the Bible to know how to respond to your feelings. I want to encourage you to be stronger than your fears and do what God wants you to do: **talk with your mom**. How do I know He wants you to do that? Because this Truth Nugget says that we never outgrow the need for wise advice. ▼

 TRUTH NUGGET: "Walk with the wise and become wise; associate with fools and get in trouble." (Proverbs 13:20)

This Proverb is for you. It's for me. It's also for our moms and grandmas. It doesn't say "walk with wise people until you are 12, or 18, or 21." It just says to do it. You'll never outgrow this Bible verse.

"Walking with wise people" means including them in **all** areas of your life. That includes talking about boys. In fact, since marriage is such a big deal to God, the topic of boys may be one of the most important things to talk about.

Would it help you to know that your mom might feel a little uncomfortable about this too? For a long time, I have been helping moms and daughters talk about boys. (I believe it's **THAT** important!) One thing I recommend is starting a mother/daughter journal. This is a good way to ease into the more uncomfortable topics you need to talk about. (You can also use it with your grandma or auntie or a woman you like at church, if that's someone God has given you to talk to about important things!) It works like this:

💜 Find a spiral-bound notebook in your house. There's usually one lying around somewhere.

💜 Label it: "Our Journal." Decorate the cover and make it yours!

💜 Write the first letter or journal entry to your mom or grandma or auntie or whoever beginning with this: "*Lies Girls Believe* has taught me that you never outgrow wise advice. I want to start getting advice, and I want you to be my advisor. One thing I need to talk about is boys. Some other topics are (include some things that you need help with). Could we start writing back and forth in this journal? It might make it easier to talk." Now add to this and just write from your heart. Write two questions you have about boys. Then, sign your name.

💜 Put the notebook somewhere that your wise advisor can find it.

💜 Wait for it to show up on your bed, or desk, or workspace with a journal entry full of good advice.

This has been a really good tool for some moms and daughters who have had a hard time getting started. And, I think you'll find that it gets easier once you dive in. One girl told me:

> It's weird to talk to my mom about boys. But after you do it, you feel a lot better.

NOTES FOR MOM

Conversation Tip for Truth #16:

When my girls were tweens, I found some topics to be more challenging than others. A wise friend offered me the idea of journaling back and forth. It gave each of us the chance to check our words and avoid the risk of misinterpreting each other.

If your daughter has not already grabbed a spiral bound notebook for the suggested activity in this chapter, find one and bring some art supplies to decorate it while you talk about boys. Sometimes having the hands engaged in activity makes the conversation less awkward.

I would give your daughter the choice of whether she wants to write in the journal first, or have you take the lead. If you begin, tell her what an honor and privilege it is to be her mom and that you'd love to have her trust as she navigates the world of boys and relationships.

NOTES FOR MOM

Since the assignments for your daughter's lab work are the same regardless of the chapter content, I only provided ideas about how to interact with your daughter at the end of chapter 4. You can refer back to those "Notes for Mom" on pages 72–73 if you need a refresher.

YOUR TURN IN THE LAB

Grab your pencils. It's your turn to dig deep.

THE LIE

THE TRUTH

It's okay to be boy crazy.

• **You should not "stir up" or "wake up" love until you can make a lifelong commitment to someone.** (Song of Solomon 2:7)

• **It's better to be God crazy.** (2 Corinthians 5:13–14)

• **It may be "normal" to be boy crazy, but it is not God's best.** (Philippians 2:15)

I don't need to talk to my mom about boys.

• **You will never outgrow the need for wise advice.** (Proverbs 13:20)

• **It will get easier once you get started.**

TELLING MYSELF THE TRUTH
It's your turn to be the author!

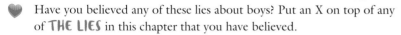

💜 Have you believed any of these lies about boys? Put an X on top of any of **THE LIES** in this chapter that you have believed.

💜 What Truth do you need to think about **all the time**, **EVERY DAY**? Look at **THE TRUTH** we dug up together. Now circle what seems important for you personally to dwell on.

💜 Next, begin to think about it **all the time**, **EVERY DAY**. You can start by writing a prayer to God, a helpful Bible verse, or some ideas you don't want to forget in the space below.

Helping Zoey Believe Truth
It's time to give Zoey some advice!

How do you think Zoey should respond to her Grandma Bing the next time she asks if she has a boyfriend? (Hint: Maybe she should get some wise advice.) Do you think that Zoey should tell her mom that her grandma is making her feel awkward? How do you think Zoey could bring the topic up?

? ? ?

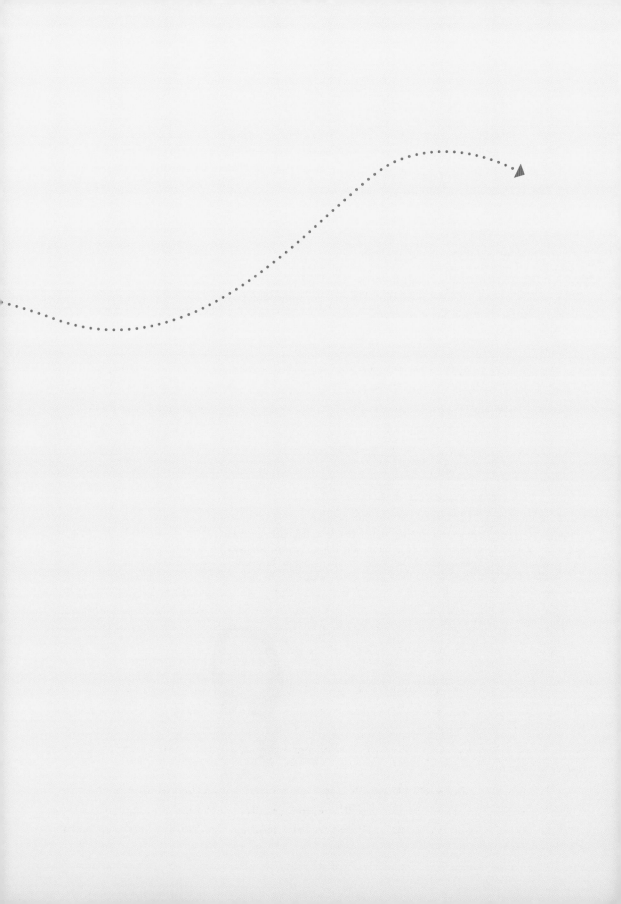

Truth and Lies about Friendship

If you asked your daughter which topic in this book is most important to her, she might answer, "Friends." So, let's explore the best way to plant Truth about friendship into our girls.

The short answer is: model the Truth for them.

Even as adult women, this can be hard. Getting picked on by the popular girl is supposed to end in middle school, but we all know that sometimes grown women don't play nice. Mommy wars are alive and well. Some women criticize the parenting choices of other moms behind their backs, while others post snarky comments for everyone to see on social media. Mothers adamantly disagree on topics ranging from breastfeeding to birth control to vaccinations to medical decisions to educational choices. This often creates division in neighborhoods, churches, and circles of friends.

Maybe you've encountered one of these women. Maybe you are one.

But mean girls don't stop there. Many of us have experienced discord in our own families because of them. Maybe it's your grandmother and your mom, or two sisters. Before you know it, a small miscommunication or lack of understanding becomes a lifelong standoff. The conflict may result in families not talking to each other, spending holidays apart, or not helping each other in times of need. When women allow their inner mean-girl to come out, it can be incredibly destructive to families and other relationships.

Let's look at the classic mean-girl narrative of the Bible: Sarai and Hagar. The story is found in Genesis 16.

Sarai wasn't able to have children. Because she knew this was a top priority for her husband, Abram, Sarai instructed him to marry and have a child with her maid, Hagar. (Let me just say, I'm so thankful that our culture today generally observes biblical instruction for men to have only one wife. This family may have been choosing what was normal for their world, but it was not God's design.)

The Bible says that "when Hagar knew she was pregnant, she began to treat her mistress, Sarai, with contempt" (Genesis 16:4). With her new position and successful pregnancy, Hagar thought Sarai was of no importance. Of course, Sarai returned the disdain and treated Hagar equally poorly.

Can you imagine the pain? You and I may never know a relationship as complicated as the one these poor women shared. They were having sex with the same man. The insecurities, bitterness, and shame must have been piled so deep that only God Himself could rescue them. And He does rescue them, as Scripture later explains. But for now, let's look at how these two mean girls made matters worse.

Instead of caring about each other's pain, these women allowed an inflated view of themselves and reactive self-protection to impact their difficult situation further. It became a personal feud that was destructive to the entire family. In the end, Hagar and her son Ishmael are cut off from everyone and everything they'd ever known. God does show up to comfort and provide for them, but no thanks to Sarai.

Since I have witnessed modern-day estrangements in families, I sometimes wonder: *Did these women ever miss the fellowship they once shared? Did Isaac long for his big brother, Ishmael? Was Sarai's relationship with Abram ever the same, or did he feel controlled by his first wife's bitterness?* The implications impacted everyone, not just Sarai and Hagar.

The way we treat others affects everyone around us, especially our children. If they see a mean girl in us, they will likely copy our behavior. However, if they find us loving others, they will do likewise. Let's set a Truth-fueled example. God's Word prescribes this: ▼

TRUTH NUGGET: "Don't be selfish; don't try to impress others. Be humble, thinking of others as better than yourselves. Don't look out only for your own interests, but take an interest in others, too." (Philippians 2:3–4)

I find that thinking of others as better than myself keeps self-centeredness at bay. This is particularly helpful when I can't see someone else's point of view. When you model this, your daughter has a better shot at having healthy friendships.

Another area we need to model for our girls is how to put friendships in general into proper perspective. It didn't matter what topic we discussed in the moms' focus groups, it often ended up circling back to mean girls, frenemies, best friends, and bullies. While I realize this reflects how complicated our daughters' friendships often are during the tween years, I sensed that some of the moms were placing the wrong emphasis on having friends. This conclusion was most apparent to me when we talked about church. Moms said things like this:

- *Church is just a place for my daughter to find friends.*

- *Friendships for my daughter are a top consideration when we select a church.*

- *The most important part about church is good friendships because they will positively influence my daughter.*

It's true that positive peer pressure is a good thing to want for your daughter. It's even true that we all need faithful friends. But, I was uncomfortable with how quickly the conversation became emotional when we started discussing friends at church. It seemed to me that while many of these moms were being wise stewards of their daughter's relationships, some of their hearts were literally breaking with and for their girls when the topic came up. That is certainly something I have experienced. Let me give you two pieces of advice.

1 **Model biblical friendship.** I guess I've already said this, but sometimes a basic truth begs to be repeated. We simply must model biblical friendship. In your daughter's book I have included six factors of true friendship. As you read over this content, consider whether or not you are modeling these biblical qualities with your own relationships. That will go a long way to help your daughter have healthy friendships.

2 **Create opportunities for your daughter to talk about what's wrong in her relationships.** I know it breaks your heart when your girl experiences mean-girl moments, frenemies, or bullying. You may even be tempted to avoid the conversation because it just hurts too much. Trust me. I understand. But the best way you can help her is to create opportunities for her to tell you when she experiences these painful things.

In general, kids don't talk to adults about bullying. This includes their parents, counselors, teachers, coaches, and youth leaders. You need to become a detective, sorting out clues that your daughter may be the victim of a mean girl. And you need to be brave enough to acknowledge clues that reveal that she may be the one being mean. Such was the case of Josolyn.

A CASE STUDY: JOSOLYN

Josolyn spends half of her time in her Christian mom's home, and half of her time in her biological father's. Her mom encourages controlled behavior, but her father tells her that it is healthy to express her anger. Her mom knew about the conflict in parenting philosophy, but had no idea just how much her daughter had begun to believe what her father was teaching her.

It all came to a head one day at school. A girl who had been bullying Josolyn teased her on the playground. That was the straw that broke the camel's back for Josolyn, who reacted in a torrent of rage and violence. She grabbed her bully by the hair and drug her across the playground. She was just about to hit her with a stick, but a teacher intervened.

Her mom said, "It was chilling to watch the school playground surveillance footage and see your daughter doing something so horrific."

Josolyn's mom asked me to tell you to be brave and be willing to look at the clues in your daughter's life when she is being mean. She begged me to encourage you to ask your daughter regularly if she is being bullied, or struggling with being mean. She believes that if she had known how bad it was, she may have been able to help Josolyn before she did irreparable damage. As it ended up, she had to move her daughter to another school so she could get a fresh start.

Slow down. Ask the hard questions.

TALKING WITH GOD:

Use Philippians 2:3–4 to evaluate the way you and your daughter pursue friendships. Just look through the verse and ask yourself questions based on the instruction. Are you selfish? Do you try to impress others, or is humility present in your interactions? Do you think much of others and less of yourself? Are you tending to the needs of others or mostly your own? Take time for honest reflection, then ask God what you need to do to align your friendships with His Truth. Write out your prayer in the lines below.

> *Don't be selfish; don't try to impress others. Be humble, thinking of others as better than yourselves. Don't look out only for your own interests, but take an interest in others, too.* (Philippians 2:3–4)

_____

_____

_____

_____

_____

TALKING WITH YOUR GIRL:

Now that you've prayed, invite your daughter to read chapter 10 in her book while you review the same content right here. I've written a few notes for you in the margins. You might want to add some of your own to help prompt you when it's time to discuss this chapter with your girl.

Lies about Friendship

CHAPTER
10

I'm so **MAD AT GIGI. AGAIN!** She told me she "has no friends." Today at lunch, she told me she's going to sit with "Danika and them" from now on! Via and I sat alone. And Via had the guts to tell me that maybe I should worry less about how much I'm going to miss Gigi!!! She said that we should think about how we can help her, because she's worried about why she would do something like this.

Zoey is having a bad friend day. Have you ever had one of those? Not a surprise. Pretty much everyone in the girl world has had a bad friend day.

In fact, the stories in the Bible prove one thing about friendship. It's hard! Job's life was falling apart, and his three best friends made his pain even worse.[2] The first Christians fought so much that they decided not to work together, and started different ministries and churches.[3] Even two of Jesus' closest friends—Judas **and** Peter— were unfaithful to Him before He died![4]

NOTES FOR MOM

About Truth #17:

Many girls go through a period where they feel as if they "don't have any friends." That may be true at times. But, generally it is a result of being more focused on self than others, because it's a desire to *have* friends rather than *be* a friend. Let's tackle this.

You may recognize the story in this chapter about Laura and Katrina. I shared it as a case study earlier in this book. It seemed like the right story to illustrate healthy confrontation for your daughter, so I included a condensed version of it in this chapter of her book. I hope that reading it will help her open up to you about friendship drama, or perhaps even being bullied.

Forty-eight percent of the girls who took our survey said that they had been bullied. About 9 percent of them have never told anyone about it. Don't pry, but open the door for your daughter to have a revealing conversation with you about any ways others have wounded her. Knowing about the pain will give you the tools to help her interpret and respond to it well, just as Laura's mom did.

If your friendships aren't perfect, join the rest of the world! There's no such thing as a perfect friend. But God wants us to keep learning. Even though the Bible reminds us that friendship can be difficult, it also offers us a lot of advice about how to do it well. One thing it tells us is this:

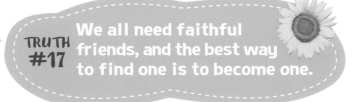

TRUTH #17

We all need faithful friends, and the best way to find one is to become one.

In an earlier chapter, we talked about how we were created to be a little bit like God. That is to say, we were created in His likeness or image. God the Father, God the Son, and God the Holy Spirit enjoy communicating with each other. You and I were created to be like that, too. So that desire you have for deep, real, true, amazing friendship is just another reminder that you were created to be like God. You need friendships, and were made to experience them.

That's why it makes me so sad when girls like you believe this lie.

▶ **LIE: "I DON'T HAVE ANY FRIENDS."** ◀

It may be true that you don't have a BFF that you hang out with, or that you aren't the most popular girl in your grade. It may be true that you just moved to a new place, and haven't met anyone yet. It may even be true that you've just had a bad friend day **TODAY**! But is it **really** true that you don't have **ANY** friends?

Before you answer that question, let me ask you another one: **what is a friend**? Obviously, a friend is someone you hang out with. The Bible has a lot to say about what makes someone a true friend. Here are five things it tells us are the differences between a frenemy—someone who is a friend one day and an enemy the next—and a true friend.

SIX FACTORS OF TRUE FRIENDSHIP

"FRENEMIES"

1. Love when it's convenient.

2. Hang around when it's good for them.

3. Lead others to make decisions that cause harm.

4. Want to be served.

5. Focus on self, and are bothered by the needs of others.

6. Say what others want to hear, no matter how true it is or is not. They'll maintain friends at any cost.

TRUE FRIENDS

1. Love all the time. (Proverbs 17:17)

2. Are loyal and faithful. (Proverbs 20:6)

3. Offer good advice that helps you make wise choices. (Proverbs 13:20)

4. Serve others. (John 15:13)

5. Focus on the needs of others. (Philippians 2:4)

6. Speak the Truth always, even when it's really hard and might risk the friendship. (Proverbs 27:6)

NOTES FOR MOM

If you need to dig deeper, I've written a book to help. It's called *A Girl's Guide to Best Friends & Mean Girls*. The Bible-study meets narrative format of the book helps your girl explore biblical responses to things like frenemies, bullying, and even pursuing healthy friendships with boys.

Conversation Tips for Truth #17:

The goal of this conversation is to use the "Six Factors of True Friendship." The two lists compare the difference of a "frenemy" and a true friend. At the end of the chart, I ask your daughter to consider which list fits her best. Ask if she is willing to share her answers with you honestly.

One way you can encourage her to reveal her heart is to open up yours to her. Look at the behavioral patterns of "frenemies" vs. true friends. Are there any areas where you need to pursue a more biblical approach to relationships? If so, tell your daughter how you feel convicted and what you are going to do about it. Then, ask your girl if she has any areas where she would like to improve the way she thinks about friendship.

Now, I have another question: **when you read those things, were you asking yourself if you HAVE any friends like that OR were you wondering if you ARE a friend like that?**

Most of us tend to worry about if we **have** true friends, rather than being concerned about whether or not we **are** a true friend. Here's a Truth Nugget I still need quite often!

TRUTH NUGGET: "A man who has friends must himself be friendly, But there is a friend who sticks closer than a brother." (Proverbs 18:24 NKJV)

Wow! The Bible says that a person who has friends is one who has proven himself to be "friendly." In other words, they have the qualities of being a true friend. Are you a good friend?

This brings me to a really cool true story of friendship. Laura and Katrina grew up together since their moms were close friends. They had playdates since preschool.

In middle school, Katrina's parents got divorced and the girls' moms grew apart. Laura missed Katrina, but Katrina had started to be a real bully.

Laura got some good advice from her mom, and they prayed about it together. The next day Laura told Katrina, "I know you're going through a hard time. Is there anything I can do to help you? I'll do anything, but you **have** to be nice to me."

Laura was . . .

being faithful . . .

offering to serve her friend, and . . .

confronting her friend's sin.

Can you say, **"TRUE FRIEND"?**

Katrina apologized. And today the girls are good friends again.

Rather than walking around saying, "I don't have any friends," maybe you could try looking around and asking God, "Who needs a friend?"

TRUTH #18

Every word you speak and every thought you think about someone should please God.

I t's "normal" for girls of all ages—even MOMS—to have "frenemies" and occasionally to be "mean girls."

A lot of girls have experienced mean girl moments.

> 🍎 Almost half of girls who took our survey say they have been bullied. (It's probably much higher than that in other surveys.)

> 🍎 29% of girls say they have been the bully or stood by and let it happen without doing anything to stop it.

Because it's so common, a lot of girls believe this lie.

▶ **LIE: "IT'S OKAY TO BE MEAN."** ◀

Girls have always believed this lie. There are even stories in the Bible of adult women who treated each other really mean. (Sometimes girls don't outgrow being mean!) I think those stories made God really sad. I know it made the women sad, because the stories tell us so.

But, I think being mean is worse than ever. For one thing, girls use "mean girl talk" to greet each other! When they want to greet a good friend they haven't seen for a while, the might say something like, "What's Up, Ugly???!!!"

I CAN'T EVEN! STOP THE MADNESS!

Words have power. God created this earth with **WORDS**! And, if we are created in His image, our words have power too. Not as much power as His have, but still a lot.

NOTES FOR MOM

About Truth #18:

Here's a stat that'll make you want to raise a good kid. When bystanders intervene, bullying stops within ten seconds, 57 percent of the time.[1] In our survey of tween girls, 11 percent have witnessed someone being mean, but did nothing to protect the target of cruelty.

My mama's heart breaks at the thought of my daughters being the target of mean girls. I think it might hurt even more to know she was the bully. Eighteen percent of the girls who took our survey admitted that they had been a mean girl or bully. I'm going to go out on a limb here and suggest that they probably were not including interactions with siblings and parents when they selected that option. Otherwise, the percentage would have been a vast majority.

Living with kindness on our tongues does not come naturally. We are prone to say mean things, gossip, and slander. These days many girls are even using unkind curse words to greet best friends. Using foul, vulgar language in humor may be considered normal, but it is not pleasing to our heavenly Father.

God's Word says every word we speak and every thought we have should please Him. That is a high standard, but it's the one you and I need to establish for ourselves and our girls.

NOTES FOR MOM

Big Question:

When we witness bullying but say and do nothing, what does that say about the condition of our hearts?

Conversation Tips for Truth #18:

This conversation needs a thick infusion of grace. Apply it liberally.

Often, we are the targets of our daughter's bad attitudes, harsh words, or anger. At other times, her siblings may take the brunt. If we aren't careful, we default into a mother who is focused on restraining our daughter's behavior because we so badly want to see change.

Controlling her without an attempt to understand why she is using ugly words is unlikely to yield long-term heart change. Slow down. Take the time to help her figure out *why* she is mean, and *how* to adjust her heart.

Avoid pointing out the most recent time she used harsh or unpleasant language or the fact that she even has. Instead, use questions to open her heart.

"Have you ever been bullied?"

"Have you ever been the mean girl?"

"Can you identify with what it says in the Bible about the tongue being difficult to tame?"

I've never created a mountain or a star, but I have "created" friendship and courage and hope and faith with the words that I speak. I have also "created" anger and fear and sadness. Do you know what I mean? Have your words ever "created" bad feelings?

James 3 is about taming our tongues. It says that people have tamed all kinds of wild animals, birds, reptiles, and sea creatures, **BUT NO ONE CAN TAME THE TONGUE**!

Then, it reminds us that our tongues praise God, but still sometimes curse people. It says this shouldn't be how it is.

No, you can't tame your tongue, but do you know who can? God. And He has given us a lot of instruction in the Bible to help. Here's one of my favorite Truth Nuggets, because you can say it as a prayer to God. ▼

 TRUTH NUGGET: "May the words of my mouth and the meditation of my heart be pleasing to you, O LORD, my rock and redeemer." (Psalm 19:14)

If you call yourself a Christian and bless God with that tongue in your mouth, you should also use it to bless people. God hears every word you say to people, and knows every word you think about them.

That means, no more mean girls.

If you've been mean to someone like a friend or a sibling, this is a really good time to practice telling someone else about your sin. (See page 96.) Confess your "mean girl" moments to God and ask Him to forgive you. Then tell your mom. Ask her for help using words that are kind.

You know what else is important to talk about? If someone has been mean to you. Don't believe the lie that no one needs to know about it. And don't be embarrassed by it. **EVERYONE** has had moments when someone is mean to them. Could you do me a favor? Right now, I want you to go tell your mom or dad about the last time someone was mean to you. I'm pretty sure it'll make you feel a lot better! (It makes me feel better just thinking about it.)

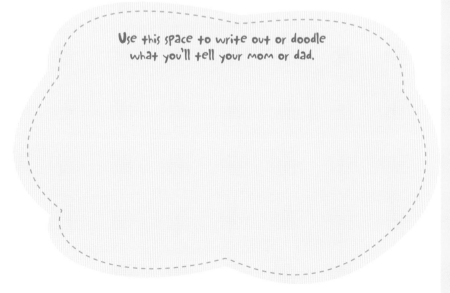

Use this space to write out or doodle what you'll tell your mom or dad.

If she does admit to being unkind, you have begun to win the battle! Confession is a big step. Remember that, and respond with tenderness as you help her to be accountable to new habits.

If she refuses to admit being mean and you feel she has a pattern that needs to be disrupted, prayerfully prepare to confront her gently. I suggest you begin indirectly with questions such as this:

"Is being mean ever okay?"

"What if someone is mean to you first?"

"Have you ever been mean because you felt someone else started it?"

This (or some other sin pattern) may be a blind spot for your daughter. Helping her see that issue may be a little bit painful, but it could save her from a lifetime of sin and broken relationships. Remember, the Bible tells us that wounds from a friend can be trusted (Proverbs 27:6).

Since the assignments for your daughter's lab work are the same regardless of the chapter content, I only provided ideas about how to interact with your daughter at the end of chapter 4. You can refer back to those "Notes for Mom" on pages 72–73 if you need a refresher.

YOUR TURN IN THE LAB

Grab your pencils. It's your turn to dig deep.

THE LIE

I don't have any friends.

It's okay to be mean.

THE TRUTH

• You need to be less concerned about having friends, and more concerned about being a friend.

• You need faithful friends, and the best way to find them is to become one. (Proverbs 18:24)

• Friendship is difficult. Even Jesus (who was a perfect Friend) had problems in friendships. (Luke 22:47–62)

• There are no perfect friendships.

• It's "normal" to be mean, but it's still sin.

• God wants you to be kind. (Ephesians 4:32)

• Words have power. (James 3:8)

• You should not praise God with your tongue, and curse people with the same tongue. (James 3:10)

• The words you say and the thoughts you think about others should be pleasing to God. (Psalm 19:14)

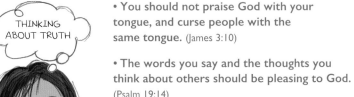

THINKING ABOUT TRUTH

TELLING MYSELF THE TRUTH
It's your turn to be the author!

💜 Have you believed any of these lies about friendship? Put an X on top of any of **THE LIES** in this chapter that you have believed.

💜 What Truth do you need to think about **all the time**, **EVERY DAY**? Look at **THE TRUTH** we dug up together. Now circle what seems important for you personally to dwell on.

💜 Next, begin to think about it **all the time**, **EVERY DAY**. You can start by writing a prayer to God, a helpful Bible verse, or some ideas you don't want to forget in the space below.

Helping Zoey Believe Truth
It's time to give Zoey some advice!

Zoey has a decision to make. Will she take Via's advice and try to help Gigi? Should she? What would you tell her to do?

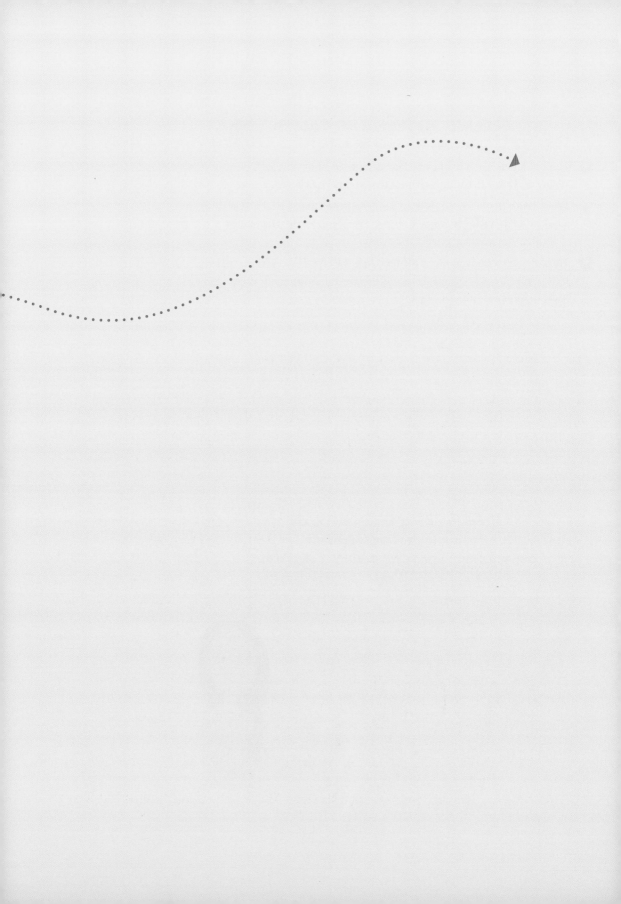

Truth and Lies about the Future

Ever since Satan tempted Eve in the Garden, he has attacked women and their God-given purposes. The feminist revolution has been a part of this assault in the West. Make no mistake: I am thankful that I can own property, vote, and earn as much money as my husband. You may be too. These are good things. And even though women now have many of the same abilities as men and virtually all of the same opportunities, I think we lost something in the pursuit of equality.

There seems to be little in our culture today that affirms a woman's choice to make being a wife and mother her sole vocation. I don't mean to say that it should be her primary goal in life. Knowing and serving Christ in any vocational pursuit is the only thing worthy of that honor. But somewhere along the way, we seem to have lost the freedom to enjoy being a wife and a mom. The attitude that an education and career are more valuable than the pursuit of a family continues to gain momentum as a cultural mindset.

As I shared in chapter 3, about 33 percent of our focus group moms were concerned that their daughters concentrated more on career goals than on family aspirations. (Let's not lose sight of the fact that these girls are ages seven to twelve, and are already considering higher education!) It wasn't that these moms didn't want their girls to go to college or even have careers someday. They did. They were simply overwhelmed by their daughters' obsessions to earn straight As, or what they perceived to be premature conversations about college and career. They also noticed that in contrast, their girls lacked enthusiasm when they tried to talk to them about the possibility of marriage and motherhood down the road.

I'm glad that I have a college degree. And Bob and I have encouraged our girls to pursue education as well. One has completed a bachelor of science degree and is considering grad school as I write this book. The other attended a Bible certification program in which she learned inductive methods of studying God's Word. She has used these skills to go through the Bible five times! It's also been a joy to watch my young adult daughters pursue the first few years of their careers.

But why can't girls and young women also love the idea of forming families? Isn't that important too?

Take a look at this verse from 2 Timothy. Read all of it—with special attention to what I've underlined for emphasis—and then I'll share with you a powerful Truth embedded within it. When I discovered this secret, it changed the way I approached planting a desire for marriage and motherhood into my girls. ▼

TRUTH NUGGET: "You should know this, Timothy, that in the last days there will be very difficult times. For people will love only themselves and their money. They will be boastful and proud, scoffing at God, disobedient to their parents, and ungrateful. They will consider nothing sacred. <u>They will be unloving</u> and unforgiving; they will slander others and have no self-control. They will be cruel and hate what is good. They will betray their friends, be reckless, be puffed up with pride, and love pleasure rather than God. They will act religious, but they will reject the power that could make them godly. Stay away from people like that!" (2 Timothy 3:1–5)

Paul urged Timothy to be watchful regarding the difficulties of the end days. He listed many negative attitudes and actions, including the fact that people "will be unloving" (v. 3). One version states that people will be "without love."[1] In the original Greek language, the word *astorgos*[2]—which refers to family love—is used to signify the type of love that's missing. In the last days, people will no longer have a love for their family or even the concept of family. They won't want to marry or have children.

Seeing this in black and white inspired me to push back against the cultural backlash that's aimed at marriage and motherhood. In response, I've done everything I can to plant the Truth that marriage is a beautiful picture of Christ and the church. It is a worthy pursuit to display that picture.

And being a mom? It's the best job I've ever had. Bar none. And I have had some pretty cool career experiences, like fighting for purity and healing on the front lines of the HIV/AIDS battle in Zambia, delivering a TEDTalk, and . . . well, writing this book for you. But nothing has compared to giving birth, cuddling newborns, witnessing my babies take their first steps, helping them do homework, watching them learn to do new things, and having three amazing young adults to set loose into this world.

Does it seem too soon to talk to your tween girl about becoming a wife and mom? If so, please re-read chapter 2. It's never too early to plant biblical Truth into your daughter.

One sign of our culture's negative attitude toward family is the rising age of marriage. In 1960, the average age of a first marriage for women was twenty. Men were twenty-two. Today it is twenty-seven for women and twenty-nine for men.[3] Two of the factors which I believe have impacted this shift are the prioritizing of education and career over marriage, as well as the devaluing of sex to the point there is no presupposition that it should be saved until the wedding night.

God's Word instructs that "two people are better off than one" (Ecclesiastes 4:9), and that we should "give honor to marriage" (Hebrews 13:4). It reads, "Children are a gift from the LORD; they are a reward from him" (Psalm 127:3). It never tells us to get graduate degrees or to make enough money to afford a big house and earn an impressive title.

To be clear, the roles of marriage and motherhood are not the only wonderful prospects that could be in your daughter's future. We are instructed to be hardworking and to please God (2 Timothy 2:15). That might be as doctors or lawyers, or teachers or mathematicians. There are endless ways your girl may end up serving the Lord and others. But that does not preclude her from being excited about becoming a wife and mother one day too, if God has that in her future. Of course, it's possible that God's plan may involve her serving Him as a single woman—whether short-term or long-term. Even so, it's okay to plant a desire in her to value marriage and motherhood.

Let's be careful to use God's Word, not our cultural mindsets, to prepare our daughters for a beautiful future.

TALKING WITH GOD:

Based on what you have just learned about 2 Timothy 3:1-5, write a prayer to God inviting Him to help you plant a love for family into your daughter. Write out your prayer in the lines below.

> *You should know this, Timothy, that in the last days there will be very difficult times. For people will love only themselves and their money. They will be boastful and proud, scoffing at God, disobedient to their parents, and ungrateful. They will consider nothing sacred. <u>They will be unloving</u> and unforgiving; they will slander others and have no self-control. They will be cruel and hate what is good. They will betray their friends, be reckless, be puffed up with pride, and love pleasure rather than God. They will act religious, but they will reject the power that could make them godly. Stay away from people like that! (2 Timothy 3:1–5)*

TALKING WITH YOUR GIRL:

Now that you've prayed, invite your daughter to read chapter 11 in her book while you review the same content right here. I've written a few notes for you in the margins. You might want to add some of your own to help prompt you when it's time to discuss this chapter with your girl.

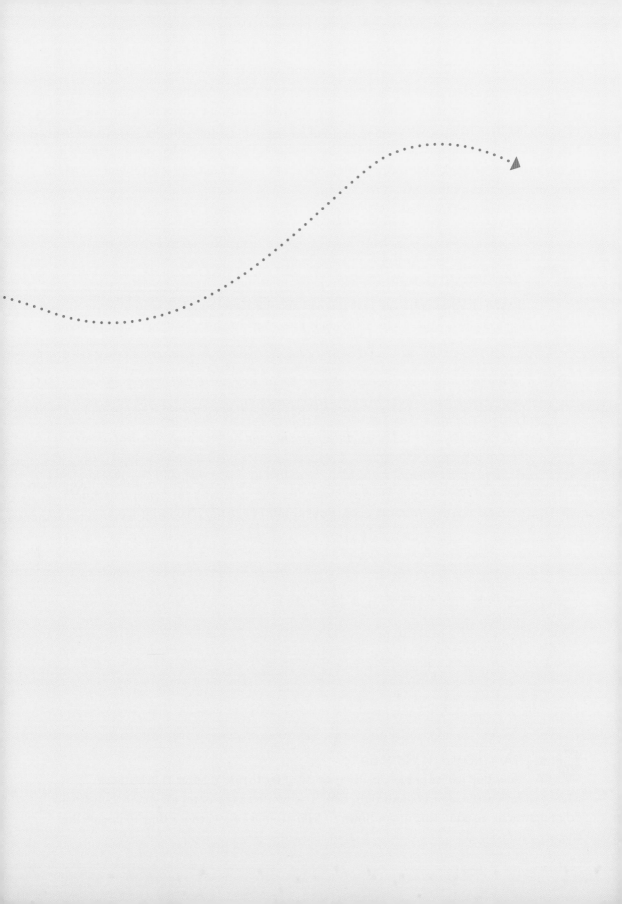

Lies about the Future

CHAPTER 11

Today Danika told us she's going to go to **HARVARD UNIVERSITY**, and own an **important science lab** some day! A lot of people laughed at her, but I think it could be true. She is like the smartest girl in the whole class. Next thing I knew, Carly said something that made people laugh even louder. She said she wants to be a wife and a mom. Someone said, "Don't you know you're supposed to want more than **that**?!" I was secretly kind of sad, **but I don't know why.**

About Truth #19

Do you ever feel insignificant in your role as a wife and/or mom? If so, your daughter will sense that, and it may impact how she feels about pursuing these roles herself one day. Be intentional about identifying any lies you may have believed about these roles and replacing them with God's Truth.

In chapter 5 of *Lies Women Believe*, Nancy addresses this lie: *"My work at home is not as significant as the work or other activities I do outside the home."* I highly recommend you read it, if you haven't already. Her thoughts reflect Titus 2 where Paul encourages and defines biblical womanhood. Much of what he writes about references how we approach our marriages, parenting, and homemaking.

Examining this passage in the light of other Scriptures, Nancy notes a few things the Apostle was *not* saying:

He is not saying women should only work at home.

He is not suggesting women are responsible solely for all the work that needs to be done at home.

He is not prohibiting us from doing work outside the home.

He is not forbidding us from being compensated for such work.

TRUTH #19
Being a wife and mom is a good and important job.

"What do you want to be when you grow up?"

That's a question people start asking you in preschool! Well, what **DO** you want to be when you grow up? **Write your top three choices below:**

1. _____

2. _____

3. _____

You are growing up at a very interesting time in history for women and girls. You can do almost **ANYTHING** you want when you grow up. It wasn't always like this. Can you believe that **way back in the day** women could not own property, vote, or even make as much money as men!!?? It's true.

The Bible tells us the stories of lots of women who did good work—for pay or for free to help people—outside of their homes. That tells me God could be planning a career outside of the home for you in the future.

But, there's a problem: a lot of girls are so obsessed with all they **WANT TO BE**, that they don't take time to ask God what they are **MEANT TO BE**! In fact, they think one of the best jobs God meant for women to love—being a wife and mom—just isn't **that** important. Some even think it's a bad idea to make it your goal in life!

They believe the lie:

▶ LIE: "IT'S NOT COOL TO BE JUST A WIFE AND A MOM." ◀

I think this is a really big, bad lie, so I have two Nuggets of Truth for you. ▼

 TRUTH NUGGET: "Then the LORD God said, 'It is not good for the man to be alone. I will make a helper who is just right for him.'" (Genesis 2:18)

This verse tells us why God created Eve. God didn't suddenly decide to make her at the last minute. He planned her all along. But first He wanted Adam to see that he needed someone with different qualities and strengths to help him. After that, God made Eve.

Some people think the word **helper** means Eve was not as important as Adam, but they don't understand this word! The book of Genesis was originally written in the Hebrew language and not in English. The word for helper was **ezer**. In this verse, it describes Eve as Adam's helper. But, in a lot of other Bible verses, this word describes **GOD AS OUR HELPER**! This is one of the cool ways that we, as women, get to be kind of like God. (Remember that from a few chapters ago? How we were made to be like Him?)

When you think of it **THAT** way, being a helper is super important. If you have a desire to be a wife one day, it is a good desire, and you can be proud of it. It is one of the best jobs God could ask you to do!

NOTES FOR MOM

He is not implying that women have no place in the public arena.

Nancy concludes that what Paul *is* saying is this: Our homes matter. The work we do in them has eternal value.

Let's not miss the opportunity to enjoy them and use them to glorify God.

As you live this out in your own life, your daughter will have a greater desire to experience it in hers.

About Truth #19

This conversation has the potential to be a lot of fun. You can start by asking your daughter what she wants to be when she grows up. There are no wrong answers. God plants desire. So, just explore and enjoy dreaming with her.

If she includes being a wife and a mom on her list, begin to explore those topics. Ask her questions like:

"How many kids might you want to have?"

"What qualities would you like to find in a husband?"

You do not have to avoid these topics just because they are in the future. Talking about them is what gives you the opportunity to plant seeds of Truth.

If she does not include them, that is okay too. But ask her why she didn't. Use the natural flow of the conversation to share your heart and to ask her a few gentle, probing questions:

"I've really enjoyed being a mom. Is that something you might like to experience one day?"

"When I was in college, I met your dad. Being married to him is one of the best experiences of my life. Do you want to get married someday?"

Take some time to tell her why you enjoy being *her* mother. Perhaps you can share about when she was born and how that made you feel.

Big Question:

Forbes magazine says a mother should earn $115,000 a year, based on what she does, the hours she works, and the money she saves the family.[4] Pretty cool, but can it really be quantified?

The second Truth Nugget I want you to see is this one. We have already used this Bible verse to fight another lie, but I think it's worth looking at again. ▼

 TRUTH NUGGET: "Children are a gift from the LORD; they are a reward from him." (Psalm 127:3)

Everyone likes to get gifts and be rewarded, right? In this verse, children are called a "gift" and a "reward." Even so, some women don't like the idea of being a mom. Even sadder to me, sometimes when they are moms, they complain about it a lot. They don't see it as a gift or reward.

This is a big lie in our world today, and one that I don't totally understand.

When I was a girl, there were three things I wanted to be when I grew up: a wife, a mom, and a Bible teacher. And I wanted them in that order! Even though I'm also a successful author, speaker, and Bible teacher—jobs I like a whole lot—the **BEST JOB EVER** has been being a wife and a mom.

Not every woman is **MEANT** to be a wife and mom, but most are. So, I hope you can be as excited about those jobs.

Here's what I think you need to do: tell God that you want to please Him with what you become in the future. Be willing to follow His plan. He created you and He knows what you were **MEANT TO BE**! If He wants you to be a wife and a mom, I'm sure you'll be a great one. He may also want you to have two careers, like me—and He will help you have wisdom about being a wife and mom, while you also grow into the responsibility of other things. Or maybe, you won't be married and become a mom at all because God has something else in mind for you.

I know one thing, He already knows and He is already preparing you. In fact, let's talk about our last big **TRUTH**!

TRUTH #20 You are becoming what you will be.

Does that truth sound confusing? Let me explain by telling you a story. When I first visited my friend Nancy's house, I noticed an interesting piece of framed art in her living room. It was a letter she wrote when she was 7 years old. It reads:

> Dear Mommy & Daddy,
>
> On Saturday, I knew that God had touched my heart and wanted me to be a missionary for Him, and it was just as if He had stood before me.
>
> Right then I started to think . . . how a missionary would speak to people. I could just tell EVERYBODY this wonderful news. I'm so happy about it. And I just know that God has spoken to me and told me to be a missionary for Him. And I think being a missionary is the best job for me.
>
> I'm just so happy that God wants me to be a missionary for Him.
>
> Nancy

When Nancy was very young, she was already becoming what she is today: a great Bible teacher and an author who leads hundreds of thousands of women in growing closer to God. Her ministry, Revive Our Hearts, is now in many countries around the world. I think that makes her a missionary. The whole world over, women know her name and trust her. She didn't wait until she was an adult to start becoming a missionary. She started when she was 7!

NOTES FOR MOM

About Truth #20

We live in a "microwave" culture. We want it right away. Right now! The mentality that we must "have it now" pervades everything we do. One significant side effect is that the human attention span is now about eight seconds long.[5]

Succumbing to this mindset will set your daughter up for great pain in the future. How will she respond when she doesn't make the soccer team in high school? What strength of character will she lean on as a single woman, longing for a husband? How will she endure barrenness or sickness if she has not learned the practice of patience, long-suffering, and waiting on God?

One way you can prepare her is to instill in her an understanding of how what she experiences now impacts her future. Helping her build some long-term vision for the years ahead, will also help her gain perspective when she faces difficult times.

About Truth #20

If you plant a lima bean, you're going to grow lima beans. Whatever is being planted and nurtured in your daughter is going to develop into something one day. This is your chance to affirm that.

A great way to end our *Lies Girls Believe* laboratory work is to get some lima beans and plant them. The growth cycle of this plant is quick and easy. Just plop one or two seeds into a cup with some potting soil, and water daily. Soon, you will see a sprout and eventually you will see a plant. This activity is a great visual reminder for your daughter that she has just planted a lot of great Truth into the soil of her heart. And it is GROWING!

This story illustrates this simple Truth of God.

TRUTH NUGGET: "Don't be misled—you cannot mock the justice of God. You will always harvest what you plant." (Galatians 6:7)

If you plant lima beans, what do you get? Lima beans! If you plant zucchini, what do you get? Zucchini!

This Bible verse tells us that the same sort of thing happens in our character. If you are a girl who reads the Bible and prays today, you are going to become a wise woman who loves God's Word and is a prayer warrior in the future.

But . . . if you are a girl who spends most of your time on the internet, playing computer games, or watching movies, it will be hard to grow a heart that loves to read the Bible and pray. Those things are not bad, and it's okay to enjoy them sometimes. But you also need to press into growing up and growing into what God hopes you will become one day. Whether that's a loving wife and mom, a lawyer, a pastor's wife, a doctor, a missionary, or a combination of all of the above!

This might be a good time for a little Note from Nancy.

Life can't be all fun. It's important to also focus on becoming what you will be when you grow up. That might mean practicing your piano, or learning to cook with your mom. It might mean studying your Bible, or working extra hard on your math homework. Before you do something, ask yourself this question: *What will that be worth in the long run?*

Nancy

Does that sound too difficult and like it's something for older women to consider?

If so, you might be believing a lie.

▶ LIE: "I'M TOO YOUNG TO _____." ◀

This lie shows up in a lot of different ways, to keep girls like you from planting good things in their lives. Sometimes it sounds like one of these lies.

🍎 "I'm too young to read my Bible."

🍎 "I'm too young to pray."

🍎 "I'm too young to make my bed."

🍎 "I'm too young to get up early."

🍎 "I'm too young to save money."

🍎 "I'm too young to give my heart to Christ and be a Christian."

If you are reading this book, you are not too young to do any of those things. Don't fall for the lie that what you are doing today as a tween girl doesn't really matter. It does. If you are disciplined, you will become disciplined. If you are kind, you will become kind. You are becoming what you will be.

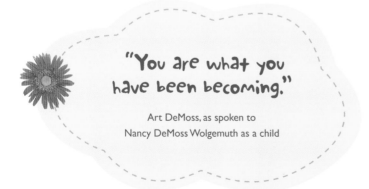

"You are what you have been becoming."

Art DeMoss, as spoken to
Nancy DeMoss Wolgemuth as a child

NOTES FOR MOM

Since the assignments for your daughter's lab work are the same regardless of the chapter content, I only provided ideas about how to interact with your daughter at the end of chapter 4. You can refer back to those "Notes for Mom" on pages 72–73 if you need a refresher.

YOUR TURN IN THE LAB

Grab your pencils. It's your turn to dig deep.

THE LIE

It's not cool to want to be JUST a wife and mother.

I'm too young to

_____.

THE TRUTH

• God created the original woman, Eve, to be a helper for the original man, Adam. Every woman has this ability to help! (Genesis 2:18)

• Children are a "gift" and a "reward." (Psalm 127:3)

• It's okay to want to have a career outside of the home if that is what you are meant to have.

• You are becoming what you will be. What you plant, you will harvest. (Galatians 6:7)

TELLING MYSELF THE TRUTH
It's your turn to be the author!

💜 Have you believed any of these lies about the future? Put an X on top of any of **THE LIES** in this chapter that you have believed.

💜 What Truth do you need to think about **all the time**, EVERY DAY? Look at **THE TRUTH** we dug up together. Now circle what seems important for you personally to dwell on.

💜 Next, begin to think about it **all the time**, EVERY DAY. You can start by writing a prayer to God, a helpful Bible verse, or some ideas you don't want to forget in the space below.

Helping Zoey Believe Truth
It's time to give Zoey some advice!

Zoey watched people make fun of a girl who wanted to be a wife and mom. Do you think it is okay for that girl to want these things? Is there something Zoey could say to her friend to make her feel better?

PART
3

the Truth That Sets Her Free

(How to Identify Lies and Replace Them with Truth)

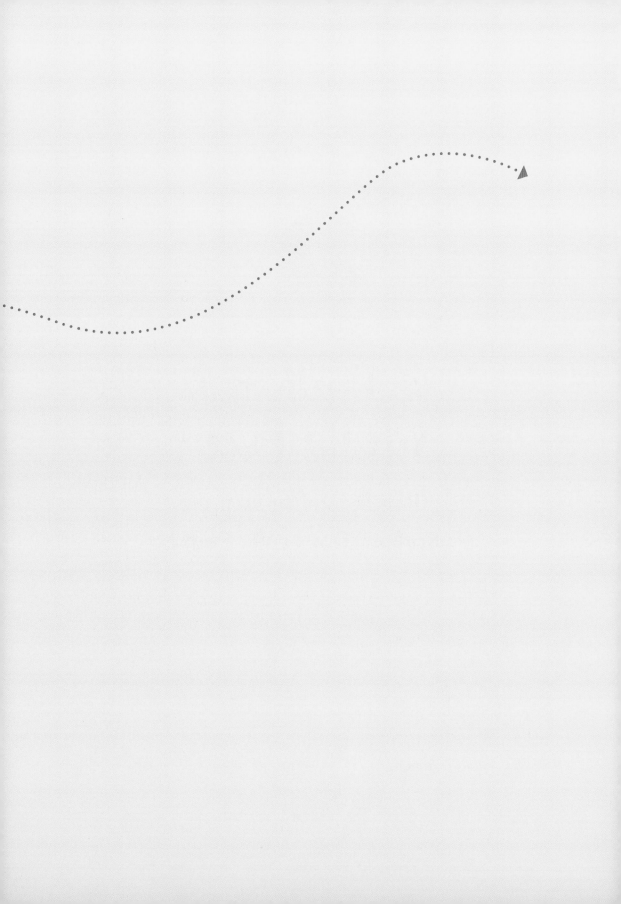

Dannah

Our time is almost up, and we haven't covered all of the lies your daughter will be tempted to believe. But don't worry. You can continue to teach her the Truth that sets her free.

A reminder: this is a process that requires much patience. While you could (and sometimes should) restrain your daughter's behavior when you see the evidence of bad roots, it is wiser and ultimately more effective to gently nurture her in grace-filled Truth. This is where it's vital to speak openly about sin and temptation, and encourage your girl to admit her failures and be involved in the process of making decisions with you about her moral behavior.

What I'm about to teach you will be time-consuming and maybe even frustrating. But the long-term outcome is worth the effort. It will produce a young woman who can make godly decisions even when you aren't nearby, because she has the roots of Truth established deep within her.

In the next two chapters, I'll teach you a three-step process to replace a lie with Truth. Then, in the final chapter, I offer a treasure trove of Bible verses for you and your girl to meditate on together.

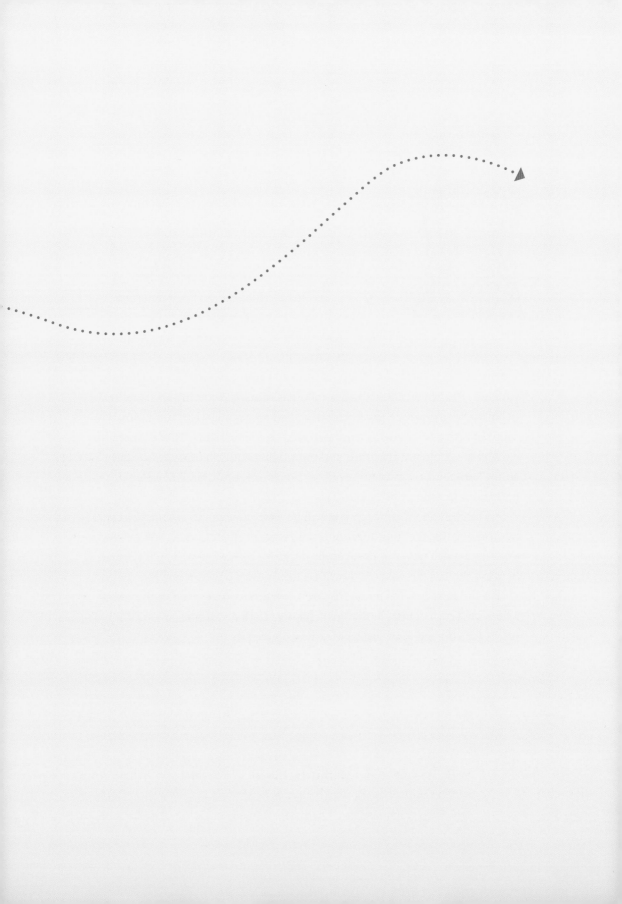

Ripping Up Roots

(How to Recognize and Identify Lies)

Honeysuckle.

Remember pinching off the end of the flower, pulling the thread-like pistil through, lifting it above your open mouth, and waiting for the sweet drop of nectar to fall on your tongue? No kid ever said anything bad about honeysuckle.

My farm has honeysuckle. Lots of it. Each spring I happily open my windows wide when the bushes explode into a gloriously sweet scent.

That is, until last year.

I began to notice problems. The trails were so overgrown with honeysuckle that I could no longer ride my horses through them. And there were a lot of dead trees. My lilac bush was struggling to bloom.

Without even realizing it, I had been lured into loving an invader. The vine growth covers trees, bringing down many of the weakest. But it's the honeysuckle roots that do the most damage. They alter soil nutrients, disrupt underground habitats for animals, and overtake entire state forests.

As I write this today, the scent of burning wood wafts into my home from a fire in the backyard. My husband has launched an ongoing war with the honeysuckle. Farmer Bob, as I call him, is not just cutting the growth off at the top. He's ripping up and burning the roots.

If you need to rip up honeysuckle roots, ask Bob.

If you need to rip up roots of untruth that have burrowed into your daughter's mind and heart, I'm your girl.

But either way, the roots have to come up, or the behaviors you don't like are going to keep coming back. Eventually, the sinfulness may overtake your daughter's life.

In this chapter, we'll dissect how to identify and uproot any lies she may believe. In the next chapter, we'll focus on how to plant Truth to replace the lies.

STINKIN' THINKIN'

So much of what your daughter believes is dependent on the thoughts she has. Her thoughts first influence how she feels, and then how she behaves. They both form and reveal the roots of her belief system.

I'm convinced that many moms would be far more careful about what their daughters see, hear, and experience, if they truly understood the power of thoughts. Relatively new medical science shows us how toxic untruthful, distorted thinking can be for any of us. (I call that "stinkin' thinkin'.") On the other hand, truthful, accurate thoughts provide an environment for your daughter to grow into a healthy woman.

Psychiatrist and neuroscientist, Dr. Daniel Amen, determined over two decades ago that treating individuals for depression, anxiety, and other emotional challenges without actually looking at the organ that controls those things—the brain—seemed like a bad idea. He pioneered the use of SPECT scans to look at a patient's brain before presumptively treating them with medication. He's seen well over 83,000 brain scans and has helped countless patients overcome a variety of painful mental health problems. While he uses modern medical interventions, diet, and exercise to help clients, he is a strong proponent of retraining the way they think.

Thoughts are powerful. They can make your mind and body feel good or they can make you feel bad. That is why emotional upset can manifest itself in physical symptoms, such as headaches or stomach aches. . . . Every time you have a good thought, a happy thought, a hopeful thought, or a kind thought, your brain releases chemicals that calm your deep limbic system and help your body to feel good.[1]

Dr. Amen believes thoughts are so powerful, that he calls the brain "the hardware of the soul."[2] That's not really news. Sometime between 700 and 300 BC, God inspired this Truth to be recorded for us in the Bible: "*as he thinks in his heart [or brain], so is he*" (Proverbs 23:7 NKJV).

Another passage of Scripture that speaks to the strength of our thought life has become quite commonly known. Dr. Amen, who is a Christian, uses it in one of his secular *New York Times* bestselling books as a prescription for mental wellness: ▼

TRUTH NUGGET: "Fix your thoughts on what is true, and honorable, and right, and pure, and lovely, and admirable. Think about things that are excellent and worthy of praise. Keep putting into practice all you learned and received from me. . . . Then the God of peace will be with you." (Philippians 4:8–9)

According to the Bible, one of the most powerful actions we can take to change our lives and emotions for the better is to think positive thoughts. When we think on things of honor, justice, purity, and loveliness, God's peace floods our being. Isn't that what you want for your daughter? To live in peace?

But let's be honest, as mothers we know this verse. We may have memorized it, hung it in our living room, and saved it on Pinterest. Yet, we are prone to allow things of dishonor, injustice, impurity, and unloveliness to assault the space in which our families live.

A picture is worth a thousand words, so let's look at the work of another leading brain specialist, Caroline Leaf, who has studied a part of the brain we can actually see. Her pioneering work caused me to take Philippians 4:8–9 even more seriously.

Dendrites are short-branched extensions of nerve cells in the brain, which send and receive impulses from other cells, helping the brain to operate the rest of the body. They are microscopic treelike structures in the brain.

Here is what they look like when we have a healthy, accurate, truth-filled thought life. The extensions are plentiful and full, creating the appearance of a strong and healthy tree.

And, here is what they look like when we have an unhealthy, distorted thought life built on lies. The extensions are few and far between and resemble dead withered branches.[3]

I don't know about you, but I want my girls to have a healthy "forest" of "dendrite trees" in their heads, not the haunted forest of negativity and lies that grows out of stinkin' thinkin'.

Though I have said it before, I feel the need to repeat an urgent plea: be careful with the thoughts that are introduced to your daughter.

Are the movies, songs, websites, friends, and classes she is exposed to filling her with Truth or lies? The thoughts that she mulls over will have a strong impact not only on her mental and spiritual values, but on the actual physiology of the brain—or hardware of the soul—which stores her belief system. Oh, please, be careful!

As I've told your daughter, "our thoughts are the boss of our feelings" which inform our behavior. So, each of us needs to decide "who will be the boss of our thoughts." Jesus wants to be.

TRUTH NUGGET: "... take captive every thought to make it obedient to Christ." (2 Corinthians 10:5 NIV)

Is Jesus in charge of the content that gets into your home and into the heart of your daughter?

I hope so.

Of course, no matter how vigilant you are, lies will get past you. So, let's get to the business of being prepared to uproot the lies and replace them with Truth. In *Lies Girls Believe*, your daughter is learning how to do just that, but she can't do it alone. No one is capable of dissecting their own lies. After all, the very nature of a lie is that it is deceptive, so it generally takes some- one else's eyes and involvement to help identify them. Your daughter is going to need your help as she learns to apply this process.

HOW TO **REPLACE A LIE** WITH THE **TRUTH**

1. Recognize the evidence. (Look for any sin or "sticky" feelings.)

2. Identify the lie and stop feeding it. (Make a commitment to stop thinking about it so much.)

3. Replace the lie with the Truth. (Find verses in the Bible to help you think about the Truth.)

Nancy

1. RECOGNIZE THE EVIDENCE

Your first task is to help your daughter *recognize the evidence* that reveals a lie under the surface. There are two kinds of evidence we visibly see: *sticky feelings* and *sin*. Sometimes you see only one, but often you'll see both.

When you notice one of these in your daughter's life, go to God in prayer and ask Him for wisdom about when and how to bring it up. Ask His Spirit to go before you in softening her heart and convicting her. He is capable of giving you spiritual eyes to see how to connect the dots from the sticky emotions and sin to any lie that may be lurking in the roots of your girl's belief system.

One mother who attended our focus groups connected the dots with a powerful moment of "Eureka!" During our conversation, she suddenly saw how her daughter's sticky feelings and sins were evidence of a lie. Here is Sophia's story.

A CASE STUDY: **SOPHIA**

Briana's daughter, Sophia, is a bright upper elementary student who has loved and excelled in school since kindergarten. Recently, however, she lashed out at her siblings if they distracted her when she was studying. On family game night, she often burst into tears if her parents made her stop doing homework to participate.

Since her grades were way above average, her parents decided Sophia's stress level about her grades was unhealthy. They established boundaries: no homework or studying after dinner. The decision was met with tantrums, tears, and frequent disobedience.

During our focus group, Briana began to realize that Sophia's erratic emotions and sinful behavior were probably the results of a lie. She even started to connect it to one role model in her daughter's life: her principal.

"Every morning during group time, the principal tells the students things like, 'Learn your math because you can't go to high school unless you do well in math. And then you can't go to college. And then you won't get a good job,'" reported Briana. "This principal is a godly woman, but I feel like she puts pressure on the kids too soon and overemphasizes the value of a career. In her attempt to help children be diligent, she is feeding a lie that the most important thing in my daughter's life has to do with academic performance and a future career." Briana left the focus group armed with the confidence to help Sophia identify a lie, and to be set free from her emotional relationship with homework.

Maybe you are already thinking of specific areas in your daughter's life where she is experiencing sticky feelings or sin. If not, don't worry. I've invited your daughter to fill in these blanks in her book and share them with you:

> 🍎 **SOME "STICKY" FEELINGS** I'm having lately include:
>
> _____
>
> 🍎 **A SIN** I committed recently or can't stop thinking about is:
>
> _____
>
> 🍎 **A DESIRE TO SIN** I'm facing a lot is: _____
>
> _____

When she brings this to you, you'll be ready to move on to the next step in uprooting a lie.

2. IDENTIFY THE LIE AND STOP FEEDING IT

After you have seen evidence of a lie, it's time to *identify the lie and stop feeding it.* You can do this by having a conversation with your daughter. If she's brought her copy of *Lies Girls Believe* to you, be willing to push pause on your "to do" list and encourage her eagerness by getting right to it!

If you're using this process to confront some concerns you have, explain to her what you have noticed. Then, ask if she is open to letting you help her *identify the lie and stop feeding it.* Since she's studied *Lies Girls Believe,* she hopefully understands how it all works. I found that no matter what age my girls were, though, walking in humility rather than a strong dose of parental authority generally yielded the best results when I approached either of them. None of us likes it when our sin or rotten emotions get pointed out. So, walk tenderly, friend! Speak softly. Inquire, and be willing to be wrong or wait until God's Spirit has done a work of softening her and making her moldable.

If she is open to it, spend a little bit of time just talking with her and then pray. Ask God to reveal to her any lie that she may believe. Let her see how you ask Him to guide you and reveal the lie, so she can learn to hear from God along with you.

The lies may present themselves and be simple to identify. Once, when I was praying with a young girl who was lonely and emotionally numb, the lie she expressed was, "No one likes me." That's a rather obvious one.

But sometimes they are quite complicated. Another teen girl, who I wrote about in *Lies Young Women Believe* (for teens), was having panic attacks and couldn't figure out what lie they were rooted in. Neither could I. It happened when she was all alone, so it logically seemed like maybe she was afraid of the dark or of being by herself. But when we prayed and asked God to help us, she realized that the first time it happened was the night her parents told her they were getting a divorce. The lie she believed was, "Everyone is going to leave me." We could not have discovered this without God's help.

Wait on Him. Be patient. Talk it out. And above all, let your daughter take the lead in sharing thoughts that might help identify the lie. When she discovers it, I have given her a place in *Lies Girls Believe* to write it:

A LIE I am believing is:

Identifying the lie is, in essence, ripping it up by the root. It no longer has anything to hide behind once it is exposed. But then, you also need to stop feeding it. At some point, you'll need to discuss a strategy for that with your girl. She must put herself in a place where she can't easily listen to it and dwell on it. For example, if she is being tempted to believe no one likes her, she is going to have to stop withdrawing from people and start to interact. So, maybe you'll help her set up some healthy friend dates soon. If she is being tempted by a certain friend to watch a television show that isn't good for her, you may need to help redirect her toward other, healthier friendships. You get the idea.

This area is tricky because sometimes you have to put your parental hat on and provide some discipline such as taking her iPad from her for a time or restricting her Netflix use. Advocating for a parenting method that emphasizes nurturing your daughter in Truth, does not mean you will not sometimes use the method of restraint. It simply means it's not the only or primary method of discipline. And, as a rule, I'd suggest that you not communicate those decisions during your prayer and conversation time. Make a mental note, but save it. If that's a little difficult for you, review the study of God's response to Adam and Eve in chapter 3. Remember, He comforts before He confronts.

Stay in a place of comfort because you're not finished yet. You need to replace that lie with some Truth.

TALKING WITH GOD:

Use Philippians 4:8–9 to write a prayer to God. Does the language and media content in your home set an example for your children to think about what is true, honorable, just, pure, lovely, and commendable? If not, what needs to be adjusted? Write your honest thoughts to God in the lines below.

Fix your thoughts on what is true, and honorable, and right, and pure,
and lovely, and admirable. Think about things that are excellent and worthy of praise.
Keep putting into practice all you learned and received from me. . . .
Then the God of peace will be with you. (Philippians 4:8–9)

_____

_____

_____

_____

_____

TALKING WITH YOUR GIRL:

After your daughter reads chapter 12 in _Lies Girls Believe_, turn to page 146 and help her work through the process of identifying a lie. Lies are difficult to figure out on our own, even as adults. I've already encouraged her to come to you for help. (She'll replace the lie with Truth in chapter 13, so we'll come back to that part of it.) You have already seen this list, but now might be the time to fill in the blanks. I've placed it here again for your convenience.

🍎 **SOME "STICKY" FEELINGS** I'm having lately include:

_____

_____

🍎 **A SIN** I committed recently or can't stop thinking about is:

_____

_____

🍎 **A DESIRE TO SIN** I'm facing a lot is: _____

_____

_____

A **LIE** I am believing is:

_____

_____

Planting Truth

(How to Replace Lies with Truth)

> ♥
> "When you are in the
> darkest place, God shines
> the brightest."

Carla, a single mom who participated in one of the *Lies Girls Believe* focus groups, started telling me her story with that beautiful sentence.

She had given birth to her daughter, Chelsey, when she was a seventeen-year-old high school student. She had been dating a boy named Brad. He was a Christian who treated her with respect and honor. But, she didn't believe she was good enough for him and ran from the relationship. Her heart was crushed. She began to soothe herself by getting into sexual relationships with other guys. And eventually, she got pregnant.

Brad quickly returned to the scene and tried to convince Carla to marry him, but she ran like a prodigal. Though she kept the baby, she continued to emotionally medicate her pain with sexual relationships. Looking back she admits:

My daughter [and I] grew up together. I was boy-crazy and yet I didn't want her to find her identity in boys the way I did.

In the dark emotional aftermath of a particularly bad relationship, Carla begged God to help her. He answered her prayers by sending a pastor and his wife to introduce her to Jesus. She told them they would have to hold her feet to the fire. So, they invited Carla and her daughter to live with them.

The couple began to show Carla that her sinful, painful behavior was rooted in lies she believed about her worth. They introduced her to Truth that would set her free, Scripture verse by Scripture verse. Slowly, her heart was transformed. The boy-craziness of her youth was replaced by a new understanding of how much Christ loved her. A new desire to live to please Him and to conform to Truth was birthed. But the impact of her old lifestyle on her daughter was apparent. Carla shared:

So many of the things my daughter struggles with go back to watching me live my life and learning from my actions. She does not submit or obey easily because she saw me live in rebellion.

Carla knew that uprooting lies and teaching Chelsey to walk in Truth would require a lot of time and effort. So she quit a job that took her away from her daughter for long days, and got a job that enabled her to work from home. This allowed Carla to be with her daughter both when she left for school and when she came home. She also started to volunteer in her daughter's classroom, allowing them to spend even more time together.

Yet what was the most significant change for this single mom who deeply desired to erase the impact of her promiscuity on her daughter? She made a personal choice not to date, despite her desire to have a life partner. It was her conviction that God was calling her to do something radical to plant Truth into Chelsey. She communicated to her daughter that promiscuity and boy craziness were results of believing lies, and she lived *differently,* praying that Chelsey would learn from her new example.

God is so faithful! When I met Carla, her then twelve-year-old was not boy-crazy like all her friends. Instead, Chelsey had grown into a God-crazy tween who was even becoming more submissive and respectful.

And there's more.

The week Carla came to my focus group was a big week. She and Chelsey were moving to Alaska. You see, that Christian boy from high school—Brad—heard that she'd finally discovered that Jesus is Truth. In the meantime, he'd become a man and a soldier who still loved Jesus—and his high school sweetheart. He came back one more time to ask her to marry him. She didn't say yes at first. She needed time to process what this would mean for her daughter and to tell Brad about her past.

"Do you understand there have been many other men in my life?" she asked him.

He knew and had a forgiving heart.

A slow, long-distance relationship began. The couple Carla had lived with gave her wise guidance. Everyone involved felt the Lord was releasing this faithful single mother to receive the gift of a husband—and a father for Chelsey.

Both she and her daughter were excited about their new adventure. I had to ask her why she would take time to drive two hours to participate in a focus group for *Lies Girls Believe,* when she was in the middle of planning a wedding and preparing for a cross-country move. She didn't hesitate:

Because I'm free! I'm totally free from the sin that had a hold on my life, and I want other moms to know that they can be free, too. It may take making some drastic decisions, but they can be free. And their freedom will dramatically increase their daughter's ability to walk in Truth.

Her countenance said it all.

She had to come . . . to tell you that you can be free and your daughter can be free, too. Tears come to my eyes again as I write this, praying that you'll feel the power I felt when she told me her story.

It's a story I've been saving because it showcases so beautifully how your quest to live in Truth impacts your daughter's. It does not matter what lies have been in your life or your daughter's. Jesus can set you free.

3. REPLACE THE LIE WITH TRUTH

In our last chapter, we discovered how to uproot a lie. Now, it's time to focus on the best part: replacing the lie with Truth.

Once again, you pray. Rely on God to take you to His Word for specific Truth. Sometimes a Bible verse comes to mind quickly when I'm praying for Him to reveal Truth; other times, I have to be more persistent in the search. But always, His Truth comes shining through when I seek it for myself, my daughters, or other women God has entrusted to my leadership.

Let me show you how Ellory's mom did this.

A CASE STUDY: ELLORY

Ellory's father left the family when she was just in elementary school. Her mom, Jill, noticed that her now middle school daughter was gravitating toward other girls who didn't have a father in the home.

At first, Jill believed this was a good thing. Then, she began to notice her daughter growing bitter and angry. Some mothers might think this was simply the next normal stage of grief in losing a dad, but Jill's discernment was on high alert. She suspected that these were sticky feelings sounding an alarm that something in the roots of her daughter's belief system was not healthy.

Through conversations, Jill came to realize that her daughter had begun to believe the lie that being angry at her dad for leaving would relieve the sadness. The voices of other girls fixating on their anger only increased Ellory's. It is true that anger distracts us from sadness, but it does not fix the problems that create it.

"It's like Satan knows to draw them to each other because they suck each other into focusing on the rejection," said Jill. "When one of their dads doesn't come to see them when planned, they *all* get mad at their dads." *(continued . . .)*

Having identified the lie, Jill found a special Bible verse for Ellory. Since her daughter seemed to be fixating on her fatherlessness, she prayerfully searched the Word of God for something about *fixating* and found this verse.

> *Let us run with perseverance the race marked out for us, fixing our eyes on Jesus, the pioneer and perfecter of faith. For the joy set before him he endured the cross, scorning its shame, and sat down at the right hand of the throne of God.* (Hebrews 12:1–2 NIV)

This verse, though not specifically about fatherlessness, is the one God's Spirit led Jill to for her daughter. It is rich with Truth that will help teach Ellory to fix her focus on God and will encourage her to embrace joy even when enduring pain.

It will not happen overnight, but Jill is ripping up the roots of the lies and planting Truth in her daughter. She can already see that joy and hope are beginning to replace the sticky feelings.

Ellory could have grown up with the loneliness, bitterness, and anger from her father's rejection and let it continue to impact future relationships. Many adult women have deep father wounds. Instead, she has a mother who is sowing seeds of contentment by helping her daughter focus on the Father who never leaves.

Note that the Truth Jill found for her daughter wasn't the opposite of the lie. Sometimes that's not the Truth we most need, even though it may be the easiest to find. That is why it's so important to rely on God's Spirit during this important work.

You can do the same thing for your daughter as you notice sticky feelings or sinful behavior manifesting in her life.

I'm guessing that you might feel a bit unsure about this process. Maybe you're feeling insecure about your ability to discern the lies your daughter believes or the Truth she needs. You may be fearful that you will get it wrong and mess up your daughter forever. How can I imagine this is the case? It takes one to know one, sister! I have spent many long months working on the pages of this book fighting similar sticky feelings.

At times, I was tempted to title this: *The Book That Didn't Want to Be Written*. I have not experienced such excruciating writer's block since I penned *Lies Young Women Believe* nearly ten years ago. I had logged two long months and countless hours before I had one single solid chapter worthy of the editing process. Oh, it had been rewritten a couple of dozen times—and trashed as many times, leaving me with a blank screen over and over again. As I attempted to catch an elusive proverbial muse, here are some of the thoughts that assaulted me when I sat down to work on this book:

- These Truths are too difficult for young girls.

- What if people I love don't like the book?

- Your writing days are over.

Fueled by lies, these sticky feelings were knocking me senseless. Not a hair of Truth was in them.

And yet, I sat with a wordless screen in front of me. So there must have been some little *t* truth—some facts to fuel those lies—in the matter, right?

That's just the thing. We are not looking for little *t* truth. We are looking for the invisible, but magnificent, powerful Truth of Jesus.

Your daughter may be suffering from leukemia or depression.

She may be the mean girl everyone's afraid of or the target of one.

She may struggle with every learning disability ever diagnosed or academic pride.

She could be boy crazy or be experiencing a gender disorder.

Maybe she's simply unkind or unmotivated.

Look beyond the little *t* truth and reach for the magnificent, powerful Truth of Jesus.

Spiritual freedom is not God miraculously removing these hardships. It is the sweet peace that comes from knowing, believing, and acting on Truth even in your pain. Jesus didn't point to circumstances, religious systems, governments, doctors, or even mothers when He promised freedom to your daughter. He pointed His followers to Himself. He said: ▼

 TRUTH NUGGET: "You are truly my disciples if you remain faithful to my teachings. And you will know the truth, and the truth will set you free. . . . So if the Son sets you free, you are truly free." (John 8:31–32, 36)

Teach your daughter faithfulness to the Truth of God's Word. That is where she will find freedom. And sometimes, it will be against all visible facts.

SOMETIMES TRUTH OPPOSES THE FACTS

With the empty screen taunting me, I leaned into God's Word each day for Truth as I wrote this book. He guided me to the book of Jeremiah, where we learn about a painful time in the history of the nation of Israel. Babylonian armies were laying siege to the city, pounding down the walls, and carrying off every soldier, leader, and thinker who could have brought any comfort. Incidentally, Jeremiah had been overlooked and was in prison in the palace court. He could have been feeling sorry for himself or fearful for his nation, but he wasn't. Instead, he kept proclaiming a message of Truth: *There's hope for your children!* (see Jeremiah 31:17).

Everyone listening thought the prophet was crazy, including his cousin Hanamel who must have been a bit unscrupulous. The guy owned a piece of land in Anathoth, Jeremiah's hometown, which he offered to sell to Jeremiah—real estate purchases being so secure at the moment and all.

Jeremiah had just cried out to God's people, "Stop your incessant weeping. Hold back the tears. There's hope for your children."

Hanamel knew a sucker when he saw one.

"Oh yeah," he said. "Well, I got some ocean-front property in Anathoth. Wanna buy it?"

What do you think Jeremiah did? I mean, no person in their right mind would enter into a real estate deal knowing that hours from now their property would belong to the enemy, right? No one would have thought less of Jeremiah for turning the offer down.

But Jeremiah bought the field!

He had heard God's Truth, and in buying the field, he proved that he believed what God had told him! And get this, God told Jeremiah to make sure there were witnesses to the purchase (Jeremiah 32:12–25). Why? Because our actions prove what we believe. Perhaps God stirred up Hanamel's mind to make this offer for the very purpose of putting some grit into the words Jeremiah was speaking.

The prophet proved what he believed when he bought that field. Often, Truth is what is unseen. Because Truth is not actual facts, but a Person. Staying connected to that Person is the key to knowing Truth

My friend, when it comes to your daughter, I want to encourage you to "buy a field." It may seem like the influence of her father who is an atheist is winning out. Perhaps you have grown weary in fighting the battle of her depression or her emotional highs and lows. Maybe you have found yourself feeling hopeless because she is the last of your children at home, and the others have all gone the way of the prodigal.

Believe the impossible.

That's what my friend Carla did. She believed God could undo all the damage she had done to her daughter through her promiscuous lifestyle. In deciding to stop dating altogether, she was "buying a field." That is, she was investing in something that seemed odd and absurd. God worked miraculously through this mother's bold obedience. Her faith inspires me to pursue Truth.

I hope she inspires you, too!

TALKING WITH GOD:

Use John 8:31–32, 36 to write a prayer to God. Are you truly His disciple? Have you remained faithful to His teachings? Do you know the freedom you are hoping your daughter will know? Talk to Him about your desire for freedom.

You are truly my disciples if you remain faithful to my teachings.
And you will know the truth, and the truth will set you free. . . .
So if the Son sets you free, you are truly free. (John 8:31–32, 36)

TALKING WITH YOUR GIRL:

After your daughter reads chapter 13 in *Lies Girls Believe*, turn to page 147 and help her work through replacing her identified lie with Truth. Be patient, but persistent as you find specific Scripture verses for her to meditate on. In her book on page 159, she'll find a list of ten places where she can put her verse or lists of verses, so she sees them often. Help her to do this, and remind her often of the Truth you discover for her.

▶ **MY DAUGHTER'S TRUTH is:**

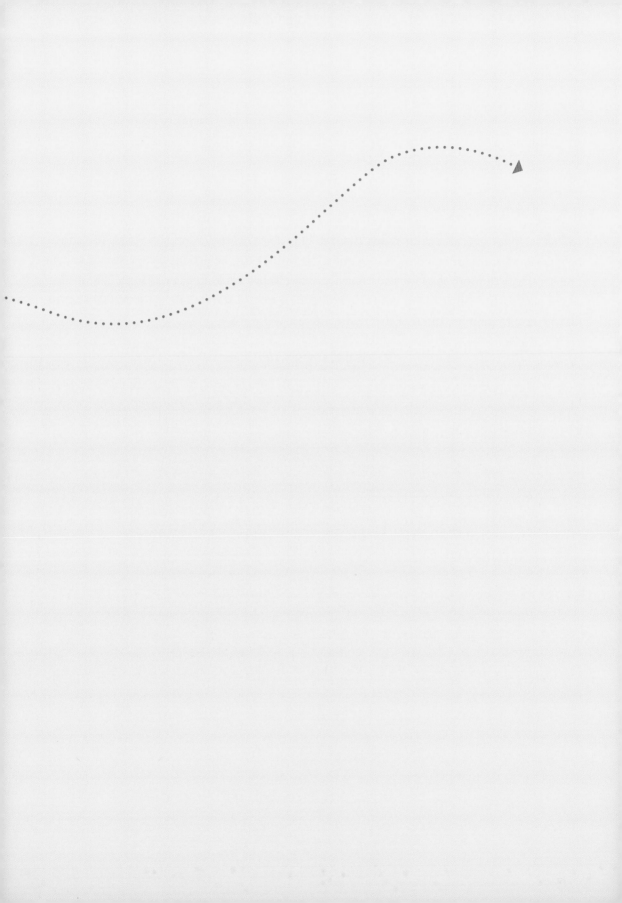

Wear a Belt of Truth

(Using Truth to Be Set Free)

I have a mother who loves her Bible and prays faithfully. When I was eight years old, she handed me my first daily devotional for children. It was the beginning of a lifelong love of reading my Bible and soaking in Truth.

As I completed research for this book, I was quite sad to discover how unusual it was for my mom to initiate an effort to encourage her daughter's devotional life. I asked the mothers who attended my focus groups if their girls were reading their Bibles and praying daily. Here's what they said:

🍎 *30% of their daughters were having a private prayer time regularly*

🍎 *48% of their daughters were not having a private prayer time*

🍎 *22% of the moms said they really didn't know the answer to the question*

While the majority of moms reported having their own private prayer time, many were not proactively helping their eight- to twelve-year-old daughters develop the skill.

We have come to the end of this book, but the work of nurturing your daughter in Truth will last a lifetime. (My mom is still nurturing me in Truth ever-so-faithfully.) So let me leave with the most important challenge of all: read your Bible and teach your daughter to read hers. In *Lies Girls Believe*, I used these words to explain to your daughter the importance of reading her Bible.

Lots of Bible verses tell us to "put on" things, like humility, righteousness, and love. Sure, you don't actually put your arms through it and put it on your body, but maybe you think to yourself: "I'm going to pick up the Truth today and wear it! I'm going to cover myself with kindness and love."

These things are spiritual characteristics that can be worn just like a pair of your favorite jeans or a team jersey! (You can't touch them or feel them, but I think you can kind of "see" when someone wears those things!) One of the things we can "put on" is the belt of Truth. ▼

 TRUTH NUGGET: "Stand up and do not be moved. Wear a belt of truth around your body." (Ephesians 6:14 NLV)

When the apostle Paul wrote this Bible verse, he also encouraged Christians to wear a bunch of other stuff like:

- 💜 the shield of righteousness
- 💜 shoes of peace
- 💜 the helmet of salvation
- 💜 the shield of faith
- 💜 the sword of the Spirit, or the Word of God

We call all these things the armor of God, and they're all important for Christians to "put on." But the "belt of Truth" is the **very first** thing Paul mentions. Why?

Well, back when Paul wrote the verses, Roman soldiers wore a belt that was a lot different from the simple leather straps we wear today.

It was a thick, heavy band made out of leather and metal, with a big protective piece that hung down in the front of it. The belt held the soldier's sword and other weapons in place.

YOUR belt of Truth holds everything else in place too. It helps you make right choices. It keeps you living in peace. It helps you keep your faith. You get the idea!!! You **have** to put it on to keep the other stuff in place. **How do you do that?**

I'm glad you asked. The answer is pretty simple.

THINK ABOUT
TRUTH EVERY DAY!

I like to do this first thing in the morning by reading my Bible and writing verses in a journal. You may find a favorite devotional book you enjoy, or maybe you'd rather have family devotions or mother/daughter devos. Maybe you will start a collection of your favorite Bible verses and tape them to your bedroom wall. It doesn't matter how you do it, but get into the Bible every single day! Each time you do, you are "putting on" the very important belt of Truth.

Putting your belt of Truth on can transform both you and your daughter.

I hope you'll continue or begin to put the belt of Truth on each morning, and that you'll help your daughter learn the same discipline. Ultimately, there is nothing better you can do to root her in Truth.

It has been my prayer to encourage you as a mom as you seek to plant seeds and nurture roots of Truth in your daughter. When we began this experience together, I wrote that you couldn't really know what your daughter's roots are made of until they're tested.

As my young adult daughters face testing of various kinds, I'm embracing this Bible verse. It is my prayer that both you and I will see it come alive in our daughters' lives. ▼

TRUTH NUGGET: "But blessed are those who trust in the Lord and have made the Lord their hope and confidence. They are like trees planted along a riverbank, with roots that reach deep into the water. Such trees are not bothered by the heat or worried by long months of drought. Their leaves stay green, and they never stop producing fruit." (Jeremiah 17:7)

My friend, may your daughter and both of my daughters be like trees planted by water. May our eyes see them walk through the testing of heat and drought. May we see them live without fear. May they live free of "sticky" feelings. And may their lives bear much fruit for God's kingdom.

20 Key Truths

At the end of *Lies Girls Believe*, I compiled a list of Truths for girls to embrace. These truths have been so helpful in my own walk, and I trust they will be helpful to both you and your daughter. (We never outgrow God's Truth.) Enjoy!

1. When you feel like God might not love you.

▶ **TRUTH:** God loves you all the time, every day, even when you have done something bad. He doesn't want you to sin and hurt because of it, but He loves you no matter what and is always ready to forgive you. (*Romans 5:8*)

2. When you feel like God is not enough.

▶ **TRUTH:** God is all you need. He is more important than friends or grades or stuff because He is the source of everything you need. (*Philippians 4:19*)

3. When you aren't sure if you are a Christian or not.

▶ **TRUTH:** You are a Christian if you have "confessed with your mouth that Jesus is Lord and you believe in your heart that God raised Him from the dead" (*Romans 10:9*). And you will be different because becoming a Christian changes the way you act. You want more of God and less of this world. (*2 Corinthians 5:17; 1 John 2:3–19*)

4. When you don't feel like you are good enough.

▶ **TRUTH:** No matter how you perform or who likes you or who doesn't like you, if you are a Christian, you have been chosen by God. On our own, we are not good enough, but with Him, we are enough. (*Ephesians 1:4*)

5. When you feel fat or ugly, and feel like pretty girls are worth more.

▶ **TRUTH:** God made you, and you are perfectly made. He didn't make any mistakes when He made you. But He is a lot less concerned with the outside of you than you are. The beauty He sees is on the inside of you and shows up as things like kindness, helpfulness, and gentleness. (*1 Samuel 16:7*)

6. When you feel like you don't have enough freedom.

▶ **TRUTH:** You don't need more freedom. You are ready for more responsibility, and God wants you to step into that. (*Galatians 6:5–6*)

7. When you feel like your family is weird.

▶ **TRUTH:** Remember that different is good. Your family is different. Every family is, and that's good. God doesn't want us to be like everyone else, but to be different because we are obeying Him. (*Ephesians 4:17, 19–20*)

8. When you feel like your family is too broken for you to be happy.

▶ **TRUTH:** God, not your family, is the source of everything. He wants to be the source of your contentment. He will teach you how to trust Him and be content in the family that you have. (*Philippians 4:11–12*)

9. When you feel like your parents don't "get" you.

▶ **TRUTH:** While it's great to get along with your parents and enjoy spending time with them, they aren't supposed to be your friends, but your parents. It's their job to set boundaries. It's your job to obey them. God will give you joy when you choose to honor your parents. (And when you're older, there's a good chance you and they will become great friends!) (*Ephesians 6:1–2*)

10. When you are tempted to believe that your sin is no big deal.

▶ **TRUTH:** All sin separates us from God, and sometimes from other people we know and love. (*Isaiah 59:2*)

11. When you are tempted to believe you don't need to tell anyone about your sin.

▶ **TRUTH:** Remember that hiding your sin sets you up for failure. You need help overcoming bad habits, temptations, and sin. Ask someone older and wiser for help. (*Proverbs 28:13; James 5:16*)

12. When you think you can watch any movie or TV show, and listen to any music you want without it impacting you.

▶ **TRUTH:** What we watch, listen to, and read changes us. It makes us believe and behave differently. God wants us to only expose ourselves to things that are true, noble, right, pure, lovely, and worthy of praise. (*Philippians 4:8*)

13. When it seems like boys and girls aren't all that different.

▶ **TRUTH:** God created two genders: male and female. They are important because they help us understand who God is, and that He is a social being. It is good to celebrate and understand the differences between boys and girls. (*Genesis 1:26–27*)

14. When you are afraid of getting your period.

▶ **TRUTH:** It's not going to be nearly as bad as you think. Every girl gets one. The best thing you can do is talk to your mom about it so you're prepared, and remember that it's a sign that your body has the ability to create life. Be thankful for this gift. (*Psalm 127:3*)

15. When everyone around you is boy crazy and you feel tempted to be.

▶ **TRUTH:** It may be "normal" to be boy crazy, but it is not God's best for you. You can say no to boy craziness. (*Song of Solomon 2:7*)

16. When you believe the lie that you don't need to talk to your mom about boys.

▶ **TRUTH:** It may be uncomfortable sometimes, but you should talk to your mom, or another trusted adult, about boys. Getting married one day, if that's what God wants for you, is a really important thing. So, talking to your mom about boys is too. Everyone needs wise advice. (*Proverbs 13:20*)

17. When you feel like you don't have any friends.

▶ **TRUTH:** We all need faithful friends, and the best way to find one is to become one. Think about how you can be a good friend, and look for people who need one. (*Proverbs 18:24*)

18. When you are struggling with being mean.

▶ **TRUTH:** Every word you speak and every thought you think about someone should please God. It may be normal to be mean, but God wants you to be kind to everyone. (*Psalm 19:14*)

19. When you think having a big career is more important than being a wife and mom, if that is what God has planned for you.

▶ **TRUTH:** It is a cool thing to be able to help a husband. Being a mom is one of the best gifts you'll ever get. (*Genesis 2:18; Psalm 127:3*)

20. When you think you are too young to start doing mature things.

▶ **TRUTH:** You are becoming who you are. If you are being kind, you will become kind. If you are being a wise girl, you will become a wise woman. (*Galatians 6:7*)

You could cut these pages out and post them in your bedroom, or write the Truths in a journal. I hope you'll use this list of Truths to "put on" the belt of Truth each day. Wear Truth! Let people see it all over you in the way you act, because the way you act is controlled by Truth, not "sticky emotions"!

I'm praying for you!

SUMMARY OF MOMS' FOCUS GROUP RESULTS*

Question 1: Do you believe that today's little girls are more prone to believe lies—about themselves, their relationships, moral behavior, and God—than you were when you were their age?

Yes 85%

No 12%

Uncertain 3%

Question 2a: What kinds of lies are you most concerned about?

Self-Esteem 32%

Faith 23%

Boys/Sex 15%

Friendship/Acceptance 11%

Peer Pressure 7%

Social Media 5%

Culture 3%

Age Compression 2%

Depression/Anxiety 1%

Homosexuality 1%

Question 2b: What does your daughter struggle with that you did not struggle with when you were her age?

Self-Esteem 23%

Physical Beauty 16%

Social Media 11%

Friendship/Acceptance 8%

Boys 8%

Homosexuality 7%

Entitlement 5%

* Not all questions will equal 100% because some chose not to answer all the questions or were given the option to answer multiple options.

Question 3: Does your daughter believe in absolute moral truth?

Responses before discussion on specific areas of motherhood/marriage and submission/obedience:

Yes 80%

No 7%

Uncertain 13%

Responses after discussion on specific areas of motherhood/marriage and submission/obedience:

Yes 56%

No 16%

Uncertain 27%

Question 3a: Does your daughter dream of/value being married and having children one day over having a career?

Yes 67%

No 18%

Uncertain 14%

Question 3b: Does your daughter display a belief in submission by the way she obeys you and other authorities in her life?

Yes, she almost always obeys 7%

No, she rarely obeys. 16%

She tries but struggles 76%

Question 4: Are mean girls, frenemies, and bullying problems in your daughter's life?

Yes 50%

No 34%

Uncertain 15%

Question 5a: Has your daughter surrendered her life to follow Christ? Is she saved?

Yes 67%

No 18%

Uncertain 13%

Question 5b: Does your daughter have her own private prayer time on a regular basis?

Yes 30%

No 48%

Uncertain 22%

Question 5c: Do you have your own private prayer time on a regular basis?

Yes 70%

No 23%

Uncertain 6%

Question 6a: Is there a part of your daughter's body or face that she does not like?

Yes 50%

No 31%

Uncertain 18%

Question 6b (only asked to those who answered "yes" to the above question): How do you feel about that part of your body or face?

I also do not like it. 28%

I have no problem with it 55%

Uncertain 17%

Question 7a: Is your daughter boy crazy?

Yes 6%

No 80%

Uncertain 14%

Question 7b (only asked to those with daughters 9–12): Have you talked to her about sex?

Yes 50%

No 46%

Uncertain 4%

Question 8: Do you believe it is possible for a little girl to be oppressed by Satan/demons?

Yes 72%

No 4%

Uncertain 23%

SUMMARY OF TWEEN GIRL SURVEY RESULTS*

Question 1: To take this survey you have to be a girl between the ages of 7–12. How do you feel about being a girl?

It's great to be a girl. 48%

Sometimes it's hard, but I usually enjoy being a girl. . . . 46%

I don't like being a girl. 1%

I don't think there is any difference between boys and girls. 4%†

Question 2: Check all the parts of your face and body that you like about yourself.

Face. 75%

Hair 90%

Skin. 69%

Eyes 91%

Weight 53%

Height. 71%

Legs 63%

Arms. 64%

None. 1%

Question 3: Check all the parts of your face and body that you do NOT like about yourself.

Face. 10%

Hair 7%

Skin. 13%

Eyes 2%

* Not all questions will equal 100% because some chose not to answer all the questions or were given the option to answer multiple options.
†The remaining percentage of girls selected "other" because none of the statements reflected how they felt about being a girl.

Weight 29%

Height. 17%

Legs 17%

Arms 12%

None. 49%

Question 4: How do you think God feels about you?

God loves me. 92%

God doesn't really love me. 1%

I'm not sure how God feels about me. 5%

Other. 2%

Question 5: Tell me about your family. Check as many of the options below that are true.

My family has too many rules. 15%

I need more freedom than my mom and dad are
willing to give me. 22%

My siblings (brother and sisters) and I fight a lot,
but that's normal. 34%

My siblings (brothers and sisters) and I fight sometimes,
butit's not okay and I wish we didn't. 47%

My family is pretty normal. 56%

My family feels really abnormal to me 11%

Question 6: When it comes to sin, check the one below that most describes what you believe.

Some sins are bigger and badder than others. 23%

All sin is equally bad and separates me from God.. . . . . 64%

I'm not sure what I believe about sin. 10%

None of the above. 4%

Question 7: When it comes to sin, do you have any secrets?

I have a secret about something bad that I did and
I have never told anyone. 15%

I have trouble with the same sin over and over again
(like lying or cheating or being a mean girl), and I have
never talked to an adult about it. 20%

I know a secret about someone else's sin and I think
I need to talk to an adult, but I'm afraid to do it. 9%

I don't have any secrets about sin. 60%

Other. 6%

Question 8: Let's talk about lying. Check any of the boxes below that are true of you.

I have a real problem with lying. I do it a lot. 12%

I don't think there is anything wrong with lying. 0.5%

Sometimes it is okay to lie, depending on the situation. . 21%

I think lying is always wrong. 55%

I don't lie very often, but sometimes I do. 58%

My parents overreact when I lie. 10%

I never lie. 4%

None of the above are true of me. 1%

Question 9: Sometimes people can be mean. Tell me about your experience with bullying. Check as many as are true for you.

I have been bullied. 47%

When I have been bullied, I have told an adult
what happened. 46%

When I have been bullied, I don't tell anyone about it. . . 9%

I have been a bully or a mean girl at times. 18%

I have stood by and watched someone bully another person
without doing anything to speak up for the victim. . . . 11%

I have seen someone being bullied, and did something
to help them. (Such as telling an adult or telling the
bully to stop.) 45%

I haven't ever seen or been around bullying. 19%

None of the above apply to me. 6%

Question 10: Tell me what you think about boys. Check anything below that you think is true.

I am boy crazy. 6%

It's okay to be boy crazy because it's normal. 11%

I have a boyfriend. 4%

My friends have boyfriends. 24%

I plan to wait until I'm older to have a boyfriend. 60%

I'm not thinking much about boys yet. 54%

Question 11: When it comes to talking to your mom about boys, how do you feel?

It's weird to talk to my mom about boys. 44%

I like to talk with my mom about boys. 19%

We don't talk about boys. 36%

Other. 15%

Question 12: Tell me what you've got. Check the boxes below if it's something you have all to yourself. (Don't include family devices that are shared or your mom or dad's.)

A smartphone with internet. 19%

A smartphone WITHOUT internet. 7%

Your own private laptop computer. 13%

Your private iPad or tablet. 37%

A TV in your bedroom 18%

An iPod or music storage device 30%

None of the above. 25%

Other 14%

Question 13: Let's talk about watching Netflix, movies, and television and listening to music. Check any of the boxes below that are true of you.

My family has too many rules about what I can
watch and listen to. 13%

My family has good rules about what I can
watch and listen to. 86%

I'm allowed to watch and listen to anything I want. . . . 3%

What I watch and listen to cannot hurt me. 15%

Question 14: If you consider yourself a Christian, what makes you a Christian?

I attend a Christian church. 13%

My mom and/or dad are Christian(s). 3%

I prayed a prayer believing that Jesus died for my sins. 69%

I was born a Christian. 6%

I am not a Christian. 2%

Other. 8%

Question 15: If you do NOT consider yourself a Christian, why?

I'm not old enough yet. 1%

I have never really thought much about it. 2%

I don't believe in Jesus. 0%

I don't really understand what I need to do to
become a Christian. 3%

I am a Christian. 93%
I consider myself to be another religion. 1%

Question 16: How old are you?

7 . . . . 8%

8 . . . . 13%

9 . . . . 16%

10 . . . . 23%

11 . . . . 21%

12 . . . . 18%

Question 17: What type of school do you attend?

Public School 51%

Homeschool 30%

Private Christian School. 16%

Private non-Christian School 1%

Other 2%

Question 18: Describe your family living arrangements using one of the options below.

I live with my mom and dad. 86%

I live with my mom only. 3%

I live with my dad only. 0%

My mom and dad live separately, and I spend time
in both homes. 2%

I live with my dad and stepmom. 0.5%

I live with my mom and stepdad. 3%

Other. 5%

THANK YOU!

Publishing *Lies Girls Believe* and *A Mom's Guide to Lies Girl's Believe* was truly a team effort, so I have some friends to thank.

Nancy DeMoss Wolgemuth patiently endured my pleas to extend her *Lies Women Believe* message to tweens. She sacrificed precious time to help direct and edit these two books. Nancy, you have become such a dear friend. You have selflessly allowed me to be involved in a line of books that God entrusted to you. I'm beside myself with gratitude and love.

Jennifer Lyell, one of the most trusted female leaders in Christian publishing and a close friend of Nancy and mine, loaned us her brilliant brain during the early stages of titling and direction. She then remained at the ready to advise. Jennifer, you have bravely fought lies planted during your tween years. Your life is a testimony of the power of Truth!

156 mothers of tweens from eleven cities in the United States and the Dominican Republic participated in our focus groups. Thank you for sharing your hearts, your wisdom, and your stories. My daughter-in-love, Aleigha Gresh, and a bonus daughter, Charmaine Porter, helped facilitate these focus groups and extrapolate the information. Thank you!

1,531 tween girls took a brief survey to cross-analyze what their mothers were telling me. Aubrey Brush, another bonus daughter and my marketing director, then helped me organize, cross-analyze, and use information accurately.

After twenty years of working together, my friends at Moody Publishers remain faithfully in the trenches of bringing Truth to the youngest of hearts. From Greg Thornton, who first gave me a chance to write a book, to Paul Santhouse, who provides wise, godly leadership to the publishing house today, your interest extends beyond my ability to create content. You have been faithful brothers in Christ to Bob and me through life's ups and downs. Thank you. Randall Payleitner, Judy Dunagan, Ashley Torres, Erik Peterson, and Connor Sterchi, thanks for being on this amazing team.

The editorial team was more significant than any publishing project I have ever completed. Ashleigh Slater, thank you for taking lead on this editing project. Your excellence to detail and theological acumen was rivaled only by your tender encouragement for this sometimes-weary author. Joy White of Cedarville University, thanks for making space in your busy world to complete a theological review of the *Lies Girls Believe* book. Michelle Burke, thank you for taking the time to review the girl's book for developmental appropriateness and even adding in your theological thoughts along the way. Mary Kassian, thanks for reviewing some of the most difficult content in *A Mom's Guide to Lies Girls Believe*. This book would not be the same without you all.

Now, isn't your daughter's book pretty? It was so important to me that it rivaled some of the bestselling tween advice books in the marketplace! Why shouldn't Jesus get the best of our design efforts! My dear friend Julia Ryan made your *Lies Girls Believe* sing with color and life and story! You are "positively" the best designer friend I have!

My ministry team at Pure Freedom were heroes and sheroes during this writing process. Wade Harris, thanks for being my advocate and helping me manage time, life, and priorities. Eileen King, you always know when to pull me aside and just pray!

My girls, Lexi and Autumn. Thanks for letting your names and hearts show up a time or two in these pages. I cannot tell you what a treasure it is to be your mother.

My mother, Kay Barker, shows up in these pages more than you would ever guess. Thank you for challenging me to have a private prayer and Bible study time when I was only eight years old.

My Bob. I love you. You have patiently endured a hard year of deadlines. Let's play a little!

NOTES

CHAPTER 1: You Have a Decision to Make

1. "Tips for Parents," Instagram, accessed May 11, 2018, https://help.instagram.com/154475974694511.

2. Juliet B. Schor, *Born to Buy: The Commercialized Child and the New Consumer Culture* (New York: Scribner, 2004), 13.

3. Kevin John Siazon,"Adolescent depression rates are on the rise with tween girls especially At Risk," Today's Parent, November 18, 2016, https://www.todaysparent.com/kids/kids-health/adolescent-depression-rates-on-the-rise/.

4. Leah Shafer, "Social Media and Teen Anxiety," Harvard Graduate School of Education, December 15, 2017, https://www.gse.harvard.edu/news/uk/17/12/social-media-and-teen-anxiety.

5. "Number of child, teen, and young adult Facebook, Instagram, and Snapchat users in the United States as of August 2017," Statista, accessed April 4, 2018, https://www.statista.com/statistics/250176/social-network-usage-of-us-teens-and-young-adults-by-age-group/.

6. Melissa Healy, "Self-harm rises sharply among tween and young teen girls, study shows," *Los Angeles Times*, November 21, 2017, http://www.latimes.com/science/sciencenow/la-sci-sn-tween-girls-self-injury-20171121-story.html.

7. Margaret Renki, "The scary trend of tweens with anorexia," CNN.com, 2011, http://www.cnn.com/2011/HEALTH/08/08/tweens.anorexia.parenting/index.html.

8. Patti Richards, "How Does Media Impact Body Image and Eating Disorder Rates," Center for Change, accessed February 12, 2018, https://centerforchange.com/how-does-media-impact-body-image-and-eating-disorder-rates/.

9. Jonathan Edwards, *The Nature of True Virtue* (Eastford, CT: Martino Fine Books, 2015).

CHAPTER 2: How to Nurture Your Daughter in Truth

1. Stuart Turton, "'Sex' makes list of top search terms for children," ITPro, December 17, 2009, http://www.itpro.co.uk/618913/sex-makes-list-of-top-search-terms-for-children.

2. SHiFT: Insights Into Winning the Battle for Our Children's Hearts, hosted by George Barna and Francis Chan (Franklin, TN: Tween Gospel Alliance, 2012), Digital video. Available at ishinelive.com.

CHAPTER 3: What's Grace Got to Do with It?

1. Dictionary.com Unabridged, based on the Random House Unabridged Dictionary, © Random House, Inc. 2018, s.v. "truth," http://www.dictionary.com/browse/truth?s=t.

2. Karl Menninger, *Whatever Became of Sin?* (Portland, OR: Hawthorn Books, 1973), 179.

CHAPTER 4: Truth and Lies about God

1. Nancy DeMoss Wolgemuth, *Lies Women Believe: And the Truth That Sets Them Free* (Chicago: Moody Publishers, 2018), 164.

2. "SHiFT," hosted by George Barna and Francis Chan (Franklin, TN: Tween Gospel Alliance, 2012), video, https://ishinelive.com/products/shift-video/.

3. Ibid.

4. Ibid.

5. Howard Culbertson, "When Americans become Christians," last updated January 15, 2016, https://home.snu.edu/~hculbert/ages.htm.

6. Barna Group, "Atheism Doubles Among Generation Z," Barna, January 24, 2018, https://www.barna.com/research/atheism-doubles-among-generation-z/.

7. Ibid.

8. Ibid.

9. Mike Nappa, "What Do Christian Teens Actually Believe About Jesus?," *Biola Magazine*, Summer 2012, http://magazine.biola.edu/article/12-summer/what-do-christian-teens-actually-believe-about-jes/.

10. This concept is updated and simplified from Philip Yancy, *Rumors of Another World: What On Earth Are We Missing?* (Grand Rapids: Zondervan, 2003), 144.

11. Philip Yancey, *What's So Amazing About Grace* (Grand Rapids: Zondervan, 2002), 70.

CHAPTER 5: Truth and Lies about Myself

1. This data represents our survey, which involved 1,521 "churched" girls between the ages of seven to twelve. Some surveys, of which included both "churched" and "unchurched" girls, found that a much higher percentage of girls did not like how they look.

2. Sadie Robertson's Facebook page, accessed January 2, 2018, https://www.facebook.com/sadiecrobertson/posts/707756299425971:0.

3. Jeffrey Zaslow, "Girls and Dieting, Then and Now," *Wall Street Journal*, September 2, 2009, https://www.wsj.com/articles/SB10001424052970204731804574386822245731710.

4. Talking with Trees, "What is Responsibility?" TalkingTreeBooks.com, accessed January 4, 2018, https://talkingtreebooks.com/definition/what-is-responsibility.html.

5. The word "tween" first made a debut in 1941, despite the fact that it was not widely used until more recently. Prior to that, the word preteen made an appearance in the 1920's. Both were words created by people who wanted to sell new products to that age group. "Tweens, teens, and twentysomethings: a history of words for young people," *Oxford Dictionaries*, accessed February 19, 2018. https://blog.oxforddictionaries.com/2015/01/13/tweens-teens-twenty-somethings-history-words-young-people/.

CHAPTER 6: Truth and Lies about My Family

1. John Piper, "Your Kingdom Come: Matthew 6:9–13, Part 1," Desiring God, Look at the Book video, 9:13, January 1, 2015, https://www.desiringgod.org/labs/your-kingdom-come.

2. Philip Yancey, *Prayer: Does It Make Any Difference?* (Grand Rapids: Zondervan, 2010), 172.

3. "What does the Bible say about contentment?," Got Questions, https://www.gotquestions.org/Bible-contentment.html.

4. Google Dictionary, s.v. "content," definition #1.

CHAPTER 7: Truth and Lies about Sin

1. Mark R. McMinn, *Why Sin Matters: The Surprising Relationship Between Our Sin and God's Grace* (Wheaton, IL: Tyndale, 2004), 110–11.

2. Nancy DeMoss Wolgemuth, *Lies Women Believe*. This quote has been modified by permission of the publisher to accommodate the reading level of *Lies Girls Believe,* but remains the same in essence.

CHAPTER 8: Truth and Lies about Being a Girl

1. Jesse Singal, "When Children Say They're Trans: Hormones? Surgery? The choices are fraught—and there are no easy answers," *The Atlantic*, July/August 2018, https://www.theatlantic.com/magazine/archive/2018/07/when-a-child-says-shes-trans/561749/.

2. Paul McHugh, "Transgender Surgery Isn't the Solution," *Wall Street Journal*, June 12, 2014, updated May 13, 2016, https://www.wsj.com/articles/paul-mchugh-transgender-surgery-isnt-the-solution-1402615120.

3. Alfred Gluckman, *Sexual Dimorphism in Human and Mammalian Biology and Pathology* (Cambridge, MA: Academic Press, 1981), 66–75.

4. Igor Klibanov, "Key Structural Differences Between Men and Women," *Fitness Solutions*, February 23, 2016, https://www.fitnesssolutionsplus.ca/blog/key-structural-differences-between-men-and-women/.

5. Christian Jarrett, "Getting in a Tangle Over Men's and Women's Brain Wiring," *Wired*, December 4, 2013, https://www.wired.com/2013/12/getting-in-a-tangle-over-men-and-womens-brain-wiring/.

CHAPTER 10: Truth about Lies and Friendship

1. "Bullying Facts and the Challenge to be Met," *Anti-Bullying Institute*, http://antibullying institute.org/facts#.WzPlRthKhQN.

2. Job 2:11–13, 6:14–27, 19:21–22, 42:7–9.

3. Acts 15:3–16:10.

4. Luke 22:47–62.

CHAPTER 11: Truth and Lies about the Future

1. New International Version.

2. *Strong's Concordance* suggests that this Greek word is specifically referring to a lack of natural affection and being hard-hearted toward kindred or family. http://biblehub.com/greek/794 .htm, accessed on July 25, 2018.

3. Eleanor Barkhorn, "Getting Married Later Is Great for College-Educated Women: For everyone else, the results are mixed," *The Atlantic*, March 15, 2013, https://www.theatlantic.com/sexes/archive/2013/03/getting-married-later-is-great-for-college-educated-women/274040/.

4. Jenna Goudreau, "Why Stay-at-Home Moms Should Earn a $115,000 Salary," *Forbes*, May 2, 2011, https://www.forbes.com/sites/jennagoudreau/2011/05/02/why-stay-at-home-moms-should-earn-a-115000-salary/#5878aeda75f4.

5. Jane Daugherty, "Living in a Microwave Society," *Whole Magazine*, October 6, 2013, http://www.wholemagazine.org/posts/olemagazine.org/2013/10/living-in-microwave-society.html.

CHAPTER 12: Ripping Up Roots

1. Daniel Amen, *Healing the Hardware of the Soul* (New York: Free Press, 2002), 158.

2. Amen, *Healing the Hardware of the Soul*, 194.

3. Dr. Caroline Leaf, *Who Switched Off My Brain?* (Southlake, TX: Thomas Nelson, 2007), 59.

Through its various outreaches and the teaching ministry of Nancy DeMoss Wolgemuth, *Revive Our Hearts* is calling women around the world to freedom, fullness, and fruitfulness in Christ.

Offering sound, biblical teaching and encouragement for women through . . .

Books & Resources Nancy's books, True Woman Books, and a wide range of audio/video

Broadcasting Two daily, nationally syndicated broadcasts (*Revive Our Hearts* and *Seeking Him*) reaching over one million listeners a week

Events & Training True Woman Conferences and events designed to equip women's ministry leaders and pastors' wives

Internet ReviveOurHearts.com, TrueWoman.com, and LiesYoungWomenBelieve.com; daily blogs, and a large, searchable collection of electronic resources for women in every season of life

Believing God for a grassroots movement of authentic revival and biblical womanhood . . .

Encouraging women to:

- Discover and embrace God's design and mission for their lives.
- Reflect the beauty and heart of Jesus Christ to their world.
- Intentionally pass on the baton of truth to the next generation.
- Pray earnestly for an outpouring of God's Spirit in their families, churches, nation, and world.

Visit us at **ReviveOurHearts.com.** We'd love to hear from you!

UNCOVER THE LIES

BREAK FREE WITH THE TRUTH

978-0-8024-1447-2

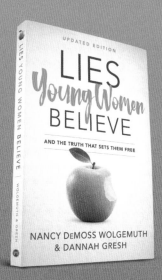

978-0-8024-1528-8

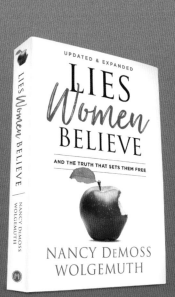

978-0-8024-1836-4

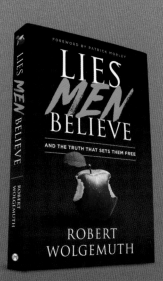

978-0-8024-1489-2

Discover the Secrets of True Beauty

For more resources and events
for tween girls, go to

MYTRUEGIRL.COM

True Girl Series

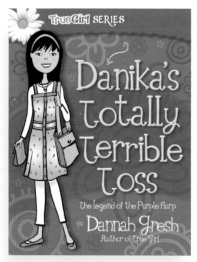

978-0-8024-8702-5

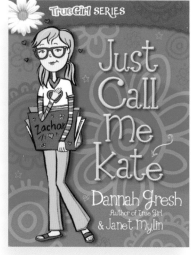

978-0-8024-8703-2

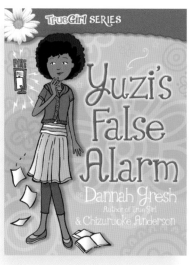

978-0-8024-8704-9

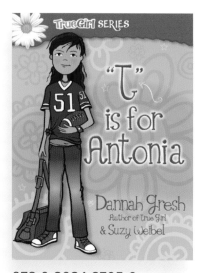

978-0-8024-8705-6

also available as eBooks

MOODY Publishers®

From the Word to Life®